Instant Vegetarian
Barbecue Ideas

INSTANT VEGETARIAN BARBECUE IDEAS

Edited by
Wendy Hobson

foulsham

LONDON • NEW YORK • TORONTO • SYDNEY

foulsham

The Publishing House, Bennetts Close, Cippenham, Berkshire
SL1 5AP, England

ISBN 0-572-02271-9

Cover Illustration by Sophie Azimont

Printed in Great Britain by
Cox & Wyman, Reading, Berkshire

CONTENTS

INTRODUCTION

There are so many vegetable variations you can enjoy on your barbecue, there's no need to be bored. Vegetables love the barbecue – and you'll love the treats you can create over the coals with these simple recipes. Mix and match, experiment to find the best combinations – there are plenty of options if you keep your eyes open for new vegetables on the supermarket or greengrocers' shelves and give them a try.

Unless you live in a place where the sunshine is guaranteed, you will want to take advantage of any good weather by having impromptu barbecues rather than planning them in advance and risking being drowned out! So lots of these ideas are simple and quick to prepare – but still give mouth-watering results.

Whether you are cooking an all-vegetarian barbecue, or making sure you have tasty vegetarian options for your family or guests, you can create colourful and interesting vegetable kebabs, tasty foil-wrapped parcels, and vegetable burgers too. Go on – give it a try!

Notes on the Recipes

- The recipes use dairy products. For vegans either omit the dairy products or use vegetarian alternatives. Make sure cheeses used are suitable for vegetarians too.

- A number of recipes use Worcestershire sauce. Traditional recipes include anchovies, so buy a vegetarian variety from health food shops.

- When following a recipe, use either metric, imperial or American measures, do not mix different sets of measurements.

- All spoon measurements are level:
  1 tsp = 5 ml; 1 tbsp = 15 ml.

- Eggs are size 3 unless otherwise stated.

- Use you favourite good quality light oil, like sunflower or groundnut (peanut) oil, unless otherwise stated.

- All preparation and cooking times are approximate.

- Always wash and peel, if necessary, all fresh produce before use.

- Where fresh herbs are used, they are specified in the ingredients. You can substitute dried herbs as long as they have time to cook; never use them for sprinkling on finished dishes. If you use dried rather than fresh herbs, use only half the stated quantity as they are very pungent. Packets of frozen chopped herbs such as parsley and mint are much better than the dried varieties.

- Always pre-heat the barbecue before cooking.

- Soak wooden skewers for about 1 hour before cooking to prevent charring.

BARBECUE BASICS

Here are some basic guidelines on getting the best out of your barbecue, and being ready to make the best of your barbecue when the weather is right!

Barbecuing is a simple technique which gives great results, but it is not an exact science. You cannot really control the temperature of the charcoal; so you must control the distance you place the food from the heat – the nearer the food to the heat, the higher the temperature and the faster the food will cook. Being a direct heat, of course, the food cooks first on the outside, so you must allow the food enough time to cook right through. This means that larger pieces of food, such as large potatoes, for example, need to be placed further from the coals, otherwise they will be charred on the outside before they are cooked inside. These principles apply whether you have a tiny Hibachi or a large gas-fired barbecue, and you will have to experiment and get to know your own equipment in order to get the best out of it. On the whole, vegetables cook very quickly on the barbecue, so there is little waiting around. They can tend to dry out more than some other foods, though, so be ready with those tasty bastes or flavoured oils to keep them moist and make sure you get delicious results.

Equipment

You can manage with your ordinary kitchen tools, of course, but if you are keen on barbecuing, it is a good idea to have a few long-handled utensils to make it easier when you are cooking on the barbecue. Have just what you need; fancy gadgets are more often than not a waste of space. Your barbecue itself can be as small and simple or as impressive as you want – it doesn't make that much difference to the taste of the food!

Most people find briquettes of compressed charcoal are the easiest fuel to use. They burn more slowly and at a higher temperature than lump charcoal, although this can light more quickly so is useful for starting the barbecue.

For the Fire

- Charcoal, firelighters, tapers, matches.
- Foil to line the barbecue (it makes it easier to clear up).
- Tongs for spreading the coals.
- Poker for flicking grey ash off the charcoal.
- Sprinkler bottle for water to douse flare-ups.
- Small shovel for adding coals and clearing ash afterwards.
- Bellows for encouraging the fire if it is dying down; blowing is hot and dirty work.
- Pile of sand for dousing the fire after cooking.
- Bucket of water just in case.
- Cleaning materials; specialist ones are available from barbecue suppliers if you find they are more effective than ordinary kitchen cleansers.

For the Food

- Tongs and spatula with long wooden handles for turning foods.

- Basting brush with long wooden handle and a jug.

- Kebab skewers; always soak wooden skewers in cold water for at least 10 minutes preferably 1 hour before use so that they do not char when cooking.

- Hinged wire grills to hold soft food between layers of mesh so that they don't break up during cooking.

- Knives, forks, chopping board.

- Foil for covering and wrapping food.

- Heat-resistant gloves and large apron.

- Trolley or small table for holding foods etc.

For the Guests

- Serving table.

- Crockery and cutlery, including serving cutlery.

- Drinks and glasses. Bottle and can openers, water jug, ice bucket.

- Tablecloth and sturdy napkins.

- Condiments and relishes.

Safety

- Set up the barbecue on a stable, level surface in the open air, avoiding any overhanging trees or nearby low bushes.

- Light the fire carefully and make sure it is always attended.

- Never move a lighted barbecue.

- Never touch any part of the barbecue once it has been lit. Extremely hot charcoal will look white and powdery rather than red hot.

- Avoid plastic or metal-handled tools as they can melt or hold the heat.

- Douse flare-ups quickly.

- Dispose of ashes carefully when they are cold.

- Immerse burns immediately in cold water and keep under water until it feels cool. Cover with a dry, sterile dressing, if necessary, and seek medical attention if severe.

Lighting and Maintaining the Fire

- Tell your neighbours you're lighting a barbecue – especially if they have washing out!

- Line the barbecue with foil, shiny side up. Open the vents if the barbecue has them.

- Arrange a few pieces of broken firelighters on the bed.

- Top with a few pieces of lump charcoal or wood chips.

- Arrange a few charcoal briquettes on top.

- Light the firelighters with a taper.

- When the charcoal has caught and is burning steadily, use long-handled tongs to spread the charcoal in a single layer, and add more charcoal at the edges.

- Gradually add charcoal around the outside of the fire to keep it at a steady temperature; putting charcoal on top will smother it. Remember that the charcoal will maintain heat for some time, so don't add more coals as you are coming to the end of cooking.

- Douse the fire with sand when you have finished cooking and leave to cool completely.

Starting to Cook

- The fire should take about 30 minutes to reach cooking temperature, by which time the charcoal will be grey and powdery. The fire is ready if you can hold your hand at about 10 cm/4 in above the coals for only 2- 3 seconds.

- Oil the grill lightly, then set it about 10 cm/4 in above the coals.

- The centre of the charcoal will always be hotter than the edges, so you can use this to good effect when arranging your food on the grill. Allow plenty of space around the foods so that you can turn them easily and they are not too crowded to cook evenly.

- Plan your cooking order in advance so that you start with the foods with the longest cooking times.

- Remember that you can arrange your dessert foods on the barbecue and watch them cook while you are enjoying your main course.

Store-cupboard Standbys

If you like barbecuing, it makes sense to keep a few things in during the barbecue season so that you can create some interesting dishes at short notice. Start with some basics, and you'll soon learn the ingredients and seasonings you use most often.

- Spices such as cayenne, cinnamon, coriander (cilantro), cumin, nutmeg, ground or fresh minced ginger.

- Dried herbs such as bay leaves, oregano, rosemary, tarragon, thyme. Prepared frozen herbs are very good, especially mint and parsley.

- Sauces such as soy sauce, Tabasco sauce, tomato purée (paste), vegetarian Worcestershire sauce, relishes and pickles.

- Seasonings such as salt and pepper (of course!), capers, sesame seeds, mustard, pesto sauce.

- Vinegars such as white and red wine vinegar, balsamic vinegar or fruit vinegars.

- Lemon juice or other citrus juices.

- Olive or groundnut (peanut) oil, sesame oil.

- Garlic, onions and fresh ginger root.

- Honey, sugar, treacle (molasses), golden (light corn) syrup.

- Canned vegetables, pulses or vegetable mixtures such as lentils, ratatouille, tomatoes.

- Canned fruits such as passion fruit, peaches.

- Crackers or melba toast.

- French or other interesting continental breads in the freezer – part-baked loaves will give you that straight-from-the-oven smell!

MARINADES AND SAUCES

If you have made a last-minute decision to have a barbecue, a marinade can help you create a whole range of different flavours with the simplest of ingredients.

Vegetables tend to absorb marinade flavours quickly, so often just a short marinating time is all that is necessary to create unusual dishes. If you have a little more time, you can leave the vegetables to marinate for a slightly longer time before barbecuing to give even more intense flavours.

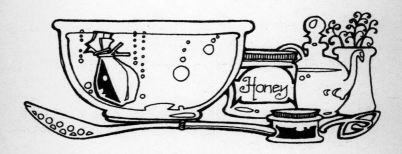

Wine Marinade

Makes about 450 ml/³/₄ pt/2 cups

	Metric	Imperial	American
Onion, chopped	1	1	1
Parsley stalks	6	6	6
Sprig of fresh tarragon or thyme	1	1	1
Bay leaf	1	1	1
Dry white wine	300 ml	¹/₂ pt	1¹/₄ cups
White wine vinegar or lemon juice	30 ml	2 tbsp	2 tbsp
Clear honey, warmed	10 ml	2 tsp	2 tsp
Oil	30 ml	2 tbsp	2 tbsp
Pinch of cayenne			
Salt and freshly ground black pepper			

Whisk together all the ingredients. Marinate foods for at least 30 minutes.

Use the marinade for firm vegetables such as cauliflower florets, onions, chicory (Belgian endive) or (bell) peppers.

Herb Marinade

Makes about 450 ml/³/₄ pt/2 cups

	Metric	Imperial	American
Lime juice	45 ml	3 tbsp	3 tbsp
Rice wine or white wine vinegar	45 ml	3 tbsp	3 tbsp
Light soy sauce	30 ml	2 tbsp	2 tbsp
Sesame oil	15 ml	1 tbsp	1 tbsp
Groundnut (peanut) oil	60 ml	4 tbsp	4 tbsp
Soft brown sugar	15 ml	1 tbsp	1 tbsp
Ground coriander (cilantro)	2.5 ml	¹/₂ tsp	¹/₂ tsp
Bunch of fresh coriander (cilantro), chopped			

Mix together the lime juice, vinegar, soy sauce and sesame oil in a glass or ceramic bowl. Gradually whisk in the groundnut oil. Stir in the remaining ingredients. Marinate foods for at least 2 hours.

This lighter marinade is ideal for vegetables such as carrots and mangetout (snow peas). Substitute 30 ml/ 2 tbsp of lemon juice if you do not have lime juice.

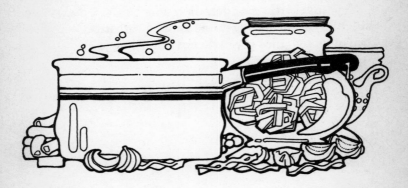

Thai-style Marinade

Makes about 450 ml/³/₄ pt/2 cups

	Metric	Imperial	American
Lime juice	75 ml	5 tbsp	5 tbsp
Sesame oil	175 ml	6 fl oz	³/₄ cup
Garlic cloves, crushed	2-3	2-3	2-3
Roasted peanuts, crushed	45 ml	3 tbsp	3 tbsp
Soft brown sugar	25 ml	1¹/₂ tbsp	1¹/₂ tbsp
Lemon grass stalk, chopped	1	1	1
Dried red chilli, crushed	2.5 ml	¹/₂ tsp	¹/₂ tsp
Chopped fresh coriander (cilantro)	45 ml	3 tbsp	3 tbsp
Vegetarian Worcestershire sauce	15 ml	1 tbsp	1 tbsp
Salt and freshly ground black pepper			

Whisk all the ingredients together in a glass or ceramic bowl and season generously with salt and pepper. Marinate foods for at least 2 hours.

Try this with mangetout (snow peas), courgettes (zucchini) or mixed vegetable kebabs. Substitute 45 ml/3 tbsp of lemon juice if you do not have lime juice.

Lemon Marinade

Makes about 450 ml/³/₄ pt/2 cups

	Metric	Imperial	American
Lemon juice	90 ml	6 tbsp	6 tbsp
Grated lemon rind	15 ml	1 tbsp	1 tbsp
Groundnut (peanut) oil	200 ml	7 fl oz	scant 1 cup
Sesame seeds	45 ml	3 tbsp	3 tbsp
Garlic cloves, crushed	2-3	2-3	2-3
Ground cumin	5 ml	1 tsp	1 tsp
Chopped fresh parsley	60 ml	4 tbsp	4 tbsp
Salt and freshly ground black pepper			

Mix together the lemon juice and rind. Gradually whisk in the oil. Toast the sesame seeds in a dry pan until golden, then crush lightly. Add all the remaining ingredients to the lemon juice and oil, seasoning generously with salt and pepper. Marinate foods for at least 1 hour.

This gives a tangy flavour to kebabs, especially those made with courgettes (zucchini).

Caribbean Marinade

Makes about 450 ml/³/₄ pt/2 cups

	Metric	Imperial	American
Canned passion fruit	400 g	14 oz	1 large can
Orange juice	120 ml	4 fl oz	¹/₂ cup
Garlic cloves, crushed	3	3	3
Dark rum	30 ml	2 tbsp	2 tbsp
Black treacle (molasses)	30 ml	2 tbsp	2 tbsp
Lime juice	60 ml	4 tbsp	4 tbsp
Tabasco sauce	5 ml	1 tsp	1 tsp
Ground coriander (cilantro)	2.5 ml	¹/₂ tsp	¹/₂ tsp
Ground cumin	2.5 ml	¹/₂ tsp	¹/₂ tsp
Chopped fresh coriander (cilantro)	30 ml	2 tbsp	2 tbsp

Simmer the passion fruit with the orange juice in a small pan for 5 minutes. Rub through a sieve. Mix with the remaining ingredients in a glass or ceramic bowl. Marinate foods for at least 2 hours. Use any remaining marinade as a sauce.

Use the marinade for fruits or sweet vegetables.

Garlic Marinade

Makes about 450 ml/³/₄ pt/2 cups

	Metric	Imperial	American
Dry white wine	300 ml	¹/₂ pt	1¹/₄ cups
Olive oil	120 ml	4 fl oz	¹/₂ cup
Bay leaf	1	1	1
Garlic cloves, crushed	2	2	2
Sugar	2.5 ml	¹/₂ tsp	¹/₂ tsp
Salt and freshly ground black pepper			

Whisk together all the ingredients. Marinate foods for at least 30 minutes. Use any remaining marinade to baste foods while cooking.

Use for any vegetables.

Rich Plum Sauce Marinade

Makes about 450 ml/³/₄ pt/2 cups

	Metric	Imperial	American
Dry sherry	30 ml	2 tbsp	2 tbsp
Oriental plum sauce	150 ml	¹/₄ pt	²/₃ cup
Soy sauce	15 ml	1 tbsp	1 tbsp
Hoisin sauce	15 ml	1 tbsp	1 tbsp
Sesame oil	5 ml	1 tsp	1 tsp
Groundnut (peanut) oil	30 ml	2 tbsp	2 tbsp
Grated fresh ginger root	15 ml	1 tbsp	1 tbsp
Garlic cloves, crushed	2	2	2
Chopped fresh coriander (cilantro)	60 ml	4 tbsp	4 tbsp

Mix together the sherry, plum, soy and hoisin sauces, and the sesame oil. Gradually whisk in the groundnut oil. Mix in the remaining ingredients. Marinate foods for at least 3 hours.

Use for vegetables such as onions or leeks. You can buy the plum sauce in supermarkets, or substitute a sweet relish.

Quick Barbecue Sauce

Makes about 300 ml/¹/₂ pt/1¹/₄ cups

	Metric	Imperial	American
Butter or margarine	50 g	2 oz	¹/₄ cup
Onion, chopped	1	1	1
Tomato purée (paste)	5 ml	1 tsp	1 tsp
Red wine vinegar	30 ml	2 tbsp	2 tbsp
Soft brown sugar	30 ml	2 tbsp	2 tbsp
Mustard powder	10 ml	2 tsp	2 tsp
Vegetarian Worcestershire sauce	30 ml	2 tbsp	2 tbsp
Water	150 ml	¹/₄ pt	²/₃ cup

Melt the butter or margarine and fry (sauté) the onion
until soft. Add the remaining ingredients, stirring together
over a low heat until well blended. Bring to the boil, then
simmer for 10 minutes.

Serve warm or cold with almost anything from the
barbecue.

Indonesian Hot Peanut Sauce

Makes about 450 ml/³/₄ pt/2 cups

	Metric	Imperial	American
Water	120 ml	4 fl oz	¹/₂ cup
White wine vinegar	120 ml	4 fl oz	¹/₂ cup
Sugar	50 g	2 oz	¹/₄ cup
Peanut butter	100 g	4 oz	¹/₂ cup
Grated fresh ginger root	30 ml	2 tbsp	2 tbsp
Garlic clove, crushed	1	1	1
Soy sauce	45 ml	3 tbsp	3 tbsp
Chopped fresh coriander (cilantro)	15 ml	1 tbsp	1 tbsp
Pinch of cayenne			
Salt			
Sesame oil	15 ml	1 tbsp	1 tbsp

Boil the water, vinegar and sugar for 5 minutes, stirring to dissolve the sugar. Remove from the heat and leave to cool. Purée the mixture with all the remaining ingredients except the oil until smooth. Blend in the oil.

Serve warm with mixed vegetable kebabs or Quorn meals.

Spicy Orange and Tomato Sauce

Makes about 450 ml/³/₄ pt/2 cups

	Metric	Imperial	American
Butter	100 g	4 oz	¹/₂ cup
Tomato purée (paste)	250 ml	8 fl oz	1 cup
White wine vinegar	250 ml	8 fl oz	1 cup
Horseradish sauce	45 ml	3 tbsp	3 tbsp
Soft brown sugar	45 ml	3 tbsp	3 tbsp
Orange juice	60 ml	4 tbsp	4 tbsp
Lemon juice	30 ml	2 tbsp	2 tbsp
Vegetarian Worcestershire sauce	15 ml	1 tbsp	1 tbsp
Salt			

Simmer all the ingredients for about 30 minutes, stirring occasionally, until thick. Serve warm or cold.

Serve with carrots or other sweet vegetables.

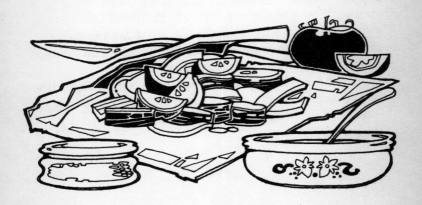

Fresh Tomato Sauce

Makes about 300 ml/¹/₂ pt/1¹/₄ cups

	Metric	Imperial	American
Oil	45 ml	3 tbsp	3 tbsp
Onion, finely chopped	1	1	1
Celery stick, finely chopped	1	1	1
Carrot, finely chopped	1	1	1
Garlic cloves, crushed	2	2	2
Ripe or canned tomatoes, chopped	1.5 kg	3 lb	3 lb
Water	45 ml	3 tbsp	3 tbsp
Pinch of sugar			
Chopped fresh basil or parsley	15 ml	1 tbsp	1 tbsp
Bay leaf	1	1	1
Salt and freshly ground black pepper			

Heat the oil and fry (sauté) the onion, celery, carrot and garlic for a few minutes over a low heat until soft but not brown. Add the remaining ingredients and bring to a simmer. Cover and simmer gently for about 20 minutes, stirring occasionally, until the tomatoes are reduced to a pulp. Discard the bay leaf. Purée the sauce, or rub through a sieve, if you want a smooth texture.

Serve hot with pasta, use in other recipes, blend into mayonnaise to make a dip, or serve as a side dressing for simply grilled vegetables.

Deep South Sauce

Makes about 450 ml/³/₄ pt/2 cups

	Metric	Imperial	American
Tomato purée (paste)	250 ml	8 fl oz	1 cup
Garlic clove, crushed	1	1	1
White wine vinegar	150 ml	¹/₄ pt	²/₃ cup
Soft brown sugar	75 g	3 oz	¹/₃ cup
Oil	75 ml	5 tbsp	5 tbsp
Vegetarian Worcestershire sauce	30 ml	2 tbsp	2 tbsp
Mustard powder	15 ml	1 tbsp	1 tbsp
Lemon juice	15 ml	1 tbsp	1 tbsp
Salt and freshly ground black pepper			

Place all the ingredients in a pan and bring to the boil.
Simmer gently for 15 minutes, stirring occasionally. Leave
to stand for 2 hours, if possible, before serving hot or cold.
Serve with robust vegetables such as potatoes or fennel.

Quick Chinese Sauce

Makes about 450 ml/³/₄ pt/2 cups

	Metric	Imperial	American
Hoisin sauce	250 ml	8 fl oz	1 cup
Rice wine or white wine			
vinegar	120 ml	4 fl oz	¹/₂ cup
Garlic cloves, crushed	2-3	2-3	2-3
Soy sauce	60 ml	4 tbsp	4 tbsp
Chopped fresh ginger			
root	15 ml	1 tbsp	1 tbsp
Anise	5 ml	1 tsp	1 tsp

Simmer all the ingredients over a low heat for 10 minutes.
Serve hot or warm.

    This sauce will keep in the fridge for several weeks in
an airtight jar. It tastes great with rice dishes.

Mustard Sauce

Makes about 450 ml/³/₄ pt/2 cups

	Metric	Imperial	American
White wine vinegar	250 ml	8 fl oz	1 cup
Made mustard	175 ml	6 fl oz	³/₄ cup
Onion, finely chopped	¹/₂	¹/₂	¹/₂
Garlic cloves, crushed	4	4	4
Water	75 ml	5 tbsp	5 tbsp
Tomato purée (paste)	60 ml	4 tbsp	4 tbsp
Paprika	15 ml	1 tbsp	1 tbsp
Cayenne	2.5 ml	¹/₂ tsp	¹/₂ tsp
Salt and freshly ground black pepper			

Gently simmer all the ingredients for about 20 minutes, stirring occasionally, until the onion is soft and the sauce thick.

Serve warm or cold with potatoes or sweetcorn (corn).

Tarragon Herb Sauce

Makes about 350 ml/12 fl oz/1¹/₂ cups

	Metric	Imperial	American
Butter or margarine	15 g	¹/₂ oz	1 tbsp
Plain (all-purpose) flour	15 g	¹/₂ oz	2 tbsp
Milk	300 ml	¹/₂ pt	1¹/₄ cups
Chopped fresh tarragon	30 ml	2 tbsp	2 tbsp
Salt and freshly ground black pepper			

Melt the butter or margarine, then stir in the flour and cook over a very low heat for 1 minute, stirring. Remove from the heat and stir in the milk until well blended. Return to a low heat and bring to the boil, stirring, then simmer gently for 2 minutes. Stir in the tarragon and season well with salt and pepper.

Serve with vegetable burgers or patties.

Treacly Apple Sauce

Makes about 450 ml/³/₄ pt/2 cups

	Metric	Imperial	American
Butter or margarine	50 g	2 oz	¹/₄ cup
Onion, finely chopped	1	1	1
Eating (dessert) apple, peeled and finely chopped	1	1	1
Apple juice	450 ml	³/₄ pt	2 cups
Black treacle (molasses)	30 ml	2 tbsp	2 tbsp
Vegetarian Worcestershire sauce	15 ml	1 tbsp	1 tbsp
Cider vinegar	15 ml	1 tbsp	1 tbsp
Ground cinnamon	5 ml	1 tsp	1 tsp

Melt the butter or margarine and fry (sauté) the onion until soft. Stir in the remaining ingredients and mix until well blended. Bring to a boil, then simmer for about 25 minutes until thickened, stirring regularly.

Serve warm with sweetcorn (corn).

Flavoured Butters

Blend any of these flavour combinations into 100 g/4 oz/
½ cup of softened unsalted (sweet) butter then roll and
chill before slicing on to barbecued vegetables.

- 1 crushed garlic clove, 15 ml/1 tbsp chopped fresh herbs
  (such as parsley, basil or oregano), 15 ml/1 tbsp lemon
  juice, salt and freshly ground black pepper.

- 15 ml/1 tbsp toasted sesame seeds (see page 32), 5 ml/
  1 tsp sesame oil, 1 finely chopped spring onion
  (scallion), salt and freshly ground black pepper.

- 15 ml/1 tbsp chopped fresh mint, 15 ml/1 tbsp made
  mustard, salt and freshly ground black pepper.

- 1 crushed garlic clove, 10-15 ml/2 tsp-1 tbsp chopped
  fresh rosemary, salt and freshly ground black pepper.

- 10 ml/2 tsp chilli powder, a few drops of Tabasco sauce,
  salt and freshly ground black pepper.

- 75 g/3 oz/¾ cup crushed almonds, plenty of salt and a
  little freshly ground black pepper.

APPETISERS

Sitting in the fresh air with the smells of the barbecue wafting across the patio is hungry business. If you make sure your guests have plenty to nibble while they are waiting for their main course, they will be less impatient, and you will be less flustered. Here is a selection of dishes you can prepare in advance to make life easy, or cook quickly at the last minute.

Marinated Mozzarella and Olives

Serves 4

	Metric	Imperial	American
Mozzarella cheese, cut into chunks	450 g	1 lb	4 cups
Stoned (pitted) black olives	75 g	3 oz	$1/2$ cup
Dry white wine	120 ml	4 fl oz	$1/2$ cup
Olive oil	120 ml	4 fl oz	$1/2$ cup
Lemon juice	30 ml	2 tbsp	2 tbsp
Sun-dried tomatoes in oil, chopped	50 g	2 oz	$1/3$ cup
Garlic cloves, crushed	2-3	2-3	2-3
Chopped fresh parsley	30 ml	2 tbsp	2 tbsp
Chopped fresh basil	30 ml	2 tbsp	2 tbsp
Pinch of cayenne			
Salt and freshly ground black pepper			

To serve

Crusty bread

Tomato salad

Place the cheese and olives in a large wide-mouthed jar or bowl. Blend together the remaining ingredients and pour over the cheese and olives. Marinate in the fridge for at least 3 hours, preferably longer.

Serve with crusty bread and a fresh tomato salad.

Sweet and Sour Tofu

Serves 4

	Metric	*Imperial*	*American*
Firm tofu	*300 g*	*10 oz*	*1 1/4 cups*
Oil	*60 ml*	*4 tbsp*	*4 tbsp*
Soy sauce	*150 ml*	*1/4 pt*	*2/3 cup*
Red wine vinegar	*30 ml*	*2 tbsp*	*2 tbsp*
Soft brown sugar	*60 ml*	*4 tbsp*	*4 tbsp*
Mustard powder	*1.5 ml*	*1/4 tsp*	*1/4 tsp*
Grated fresh ginger root	*15 ml*	*1 tbsp*	*1 tbsp*
Garlic cloves, crushed	*2*	*2*	*2*

Drain the tofu and cut into bite-sized cubes. Mix together
the marinade ingredients and pour over the tofu. Cover
and chill for 24 hours, turning occasionally. Serve with
cocktail sticks (toothpicks).

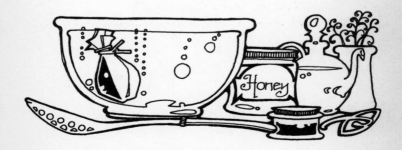

Gazpacho

Serves 4

	Metric	Imperial	American
Ripe or canned tomatoes	450 g	1 lb	1 lb
Cucumber, peeled	1/2	1/2	1/2
Red or green (bell) pepper	1	1	1
Onion	1	1	1
Sherry vinegar	15 ml	1 tbsp	1 tbsp
Olive oil	120 ml	4 fl oz	1/2 cup
Fresh breadcrumbs	100 g	4 oz	2 cups
Salt and freshly ground black pepper			
Water			
To serve			
Ice cubes			

Purée all the ingredients together until smooth. Season generously with salt and pepper. Chill well. Thin with water to the consistency you prefer.

Serve in a large tureen or individual bowls with ice cubes floating in the soup.

Chilled Spanish Almond Soup

Serves 4

	Metric	Imperial	American
Ground almonds	100 g	4 oz	1 cup
Garlic cloves, crushed	2	2	2
Water	900 ml	1¹/₂ pts	3³/₄ cups
Fresh breadcrumbs	75 g	3 oz	1¹/₂ cups
Olive oil	75 ml	5 tbsp	5 tbsp
Sherry vinegar	15 ml	1 tbsp	1 tbsp
Salt and freshly ground black pepper			

To serve
Ice cubes

Purée the almonds and garlic with a little of the water to make a paste. Mix in the breadcrumbs, then gradually beat in the oil. Add the vinegar and enough water to make the consistency you prefer. Season with salt and pepper. Chill well.

Serve in a large tureen or individual bowls with ice cubes floating in the soup.

Barbecue Idea
Of course, you can always serve a hot soup — choose something interesting and international from the chill cabinet of your local supermarket! The choice is astonishing.

Finger Foods

- Slice the top off cherry tomatoes and scoop out the insides. Stir a crushed garlic clove or two, some chopped fresh herbs, salt and pepper into a bowl of fromage frais and spoon into the tomatoes.

- Beat some snipped fresh chives, salt and pepper into cream cheese with a pinch of paprika and pipe or spread on chunks of celery.

- Serve bowls of black, green or stuffed olives.

- Cut very thin slices longways from a courgette (zucchini), then roll them round a spoonful of cream cheese flavoured with fresh herbs, a squeeze of lemon juice and some pine nuts.

- Alternate chunks of melon and pieces of fresh or semi-dried fig on cocktail sticks (toothpicks) for an interesting combination of flavours and textures.

- Spread unsalted (sweet) butter thickly on slices of ciabatta, top with sliced black olives and season with lots of black pepper and freshly chopped basil.

- Top thick slices of cucumber with a spoonful of garlic-flavoured mayonnaise (see page 108) and a sprig of dill (dillweed).

- Add a bowl or two of tortilla chips, corn chips, garlic croûtons or other inventive crackers or biscuits.

Guacamole

Serves 4

	Metric	Imperial	American
Avocados, peeled stoned (pitted) and mashed	2	2	2
Garlic clove, crushed	1	1	1
Lemon juice	30 ml	2 tbsp	2 tbsp
Olive oil	15 ml	1 tbsp	1 tbsp
Ground coriander (cilantro)	2.5 ml	$1/2$ tsp	$1/2$ tsp
A few drops of Tabasco sauce			
Salt and freshly ground black pepper			

Purée all the ingredients in a food processor. Taste and adjust the seasoning as you prefer.

Brandied Blue Cheese Dip

Serves 4

	Metric	Imperial	American
Blue cheese, grated or crumbled	100 g	4 oz	1 cup
Butter or margarine	50 g	2 oz	$^1/_4$ cup
Cream cheese	100 g	4 oz	$^1/_2$ cup
Crème fraîche	90 ml	6 tbsp	6 tbsp
Shallot, finely chopped	1	1	1
Chopped fresh parsley	30 ml	2 tbsp	2 tbsp
Brandy	45 ml	3 tbsp	3 tbsp
A few drops of vegetarian Worcestershire sauce			
A pinch of sugar			
Salt and freshly ground black pepper			

Blend all the ingredients together well and chill before serving.

Minted Soured Cream Dip

Serves 4

	Metric	Imperial	American
Soured (dairy sour) cream	250 ml	8 fl oz	1 cup
Chopped fresh mint	30 ml	2 tbsp	2 tbsp
Salt and freshly ground black pepper			

Blend all the ingredients together well, seasoning to taste with herbs, salt and pepper.

Tomato Dip

Serves 4

	Metric	Imperial	American
Canned tomatoes, drained and chopped	200 g	7 oz	1 cup
Tomato purée (paste)	45 ml	3 tbsp	3 tbsp
Chopped fresh basil	15 ml	1 tbsp	1 tbsp
A few drops of vegetarian Worcestershire sauce			
Salt and freshly ground black pepper			

Blend all the ingredients together well, seasoning to taste with vegetarian Worcestershire sauce, salt and pepper.

Herb and Lemon Dip

Serves 4

	Metric	Imperial	American
Crème fraîche	250 ml	8 fl oz	1 cup
Chopped fresh parsley	60 ml	4 tbsp	4 tbsp
Chopped fresh dill (dillweed)	60 ml	4 tbsp	4 tbsp
Snipped fresh chives	30 ml	2 tbsp	2 tbsp
Lemon juice	15 ml	1 tbsp	1 tbsp
Salt and freshly ground black pepper			

Blend all the ingredients together well, seasoning to taste with salt and pepper.

Cheese and Gherkin Dip

Serves 4

	Metric	Imperial	American
Plain yoghurt	250 ml	8 fl oz	1 cup
Strong cheese, grated	75 g	3 oz	³/₄ cup
Gherkins (cornichons), drained and chopped	2	2	2
Salt and freshly ground black pepper			

Blend all the ingredients together well, seasoning to taste with salt and pepper.

More Dip Ideas

- The easiest choice for dips has to be to buy a selection of vegetarian dips from the supermarket – and why not? There's a great range and they taste good. But they are so easy to make, and usually taste better when you have made them yourself as you can add that bit extra seasoning or interesting variation. All you need is a food processor – or you can chop the ingredients finely for a coarser texture.

- Mandarin and almond dip: mix 120 ml/4 fl oz/¹/₂ cup mayonnaise (see page 108) with 300 g/11 oz canned drained mandarins, 2.5 ml/¹/₂ tsp curry powder, 25 g/1 oz/¹/₄ cup chopped almonds and 5 ml/1 tsp lemon juice.

- Cream cheese and avocado dip: purée the flesh of an avocado with a garlic clove, 225 g/8 oz/1 cup cream cheese, 15 ml/1 tbsp lemon juice and 15 ml/1 tbsp snipped fresh chives.

- Flavour mayonnaise (see page 108), or fromage frais, or cream cheese, or thick plain yoghurt (or a combination) to taste with one of the following: grain mustard; chopped fresh herbs; crushed garlic; chopped gherkins (cornichons); tomato chutney and a few drops of vegetarian Worcestershire sauce; cayenne or chilli powder; curry powder.

Interesting Crudités

You need a choice of fresh and crunchy vegetables or biscuits to serve with your dips. Here are some ideas.

- A bowl of raw vegetables cut into thin julienne strips makes a colourful table centre and the perfect accompaniment to a selection of dips. Go for all the old favourites if you like them: carrot, cucumber, celery, (bell) peppers.

- Don't ignore other vegetables that give you a more unusual selection. Try cauliflower florets, baby carrots, sugarsnap peas, mangetout (snow peas), chicory (Belgian endive), different mushrooms or pieces of cooked asparagus.

- Fruits also offer an interesting counterpoint. Try pieces of star fruit, pear, apple, melon, pineapple, firm peach or apricot.

- Tortilla chips, corn chips and strips of pitta bread are also great for dipping.

- Try fingers of toast rubbed with a cut clove of garlic.

- Don't forget grissini, melba toast or crackers.

- Finger-shaped croûtons of bread fried until golden with a crushed clove of garlic have a wonderful flavour and texture.

Crispy Potato Skins

Serves 4

	Metric	Imperial	American
Potatoes			
Olive oil			
Coarsely ground salt			
Freshly ground black pepper			

Quantities don't really matter for this dish – just be warned to make twice as much as you think you will need – they are very moreish.

Preheat the oven to 200°C/400°F/gas mark 6. Bake the potatoes in the oven for about 1 hour or until soft to the touch. Alternatively, prick the skins with a fork and microwave until tender; 4 potatoes will take about 12 minutes. Leave to cool slightly.

Cut the potatoes into quarters and scoop out most of the insides, leaving the skins and a layer of potato. Arrange the potato skins in a shallow flameproof pan, brush them generously with olive oil, then sprinkle with lots of salt and a little pepper. Return to the hot oven for about 20 minutes, or barbecue until browned and crisp, turning and brushing again once or twice.

Use the potato flesh for: mashed potatoes; mixed with chopped onion, shaped into little cakes and fried; mixed

with cooked greens to make bubble and squeak; sliced or
crumbled into an ovenproof dish with a cheese or white
sauce, sprinkled with a mixture of grated strong cheese
and breadcrumbs and baked until crisp and golden.
Serve as a starter with dips, or as a side dish.

Fake Foccaccia

Serves 4

	Metric	Imperial	American
Olive oil	45 ml	3 tbsp	3 tbsp
Onions, sliced	6	6	6
Garlic cloves, chopped	3	3	3
Pitta breads	4	4	4
Salt and freshly ground black pepper			

Heat the oil and fry (sauté) the onions and garlic until
soft but not brown. Brush the pitta breads on one side
with a little more oil. Pile the onion and garlic mixture on
top and season generously with salt and pepper. Grill
(broil) under a hot grill (broiler) for about 5 minutes until
browned on top.

Grilled Avocado

Serves 4

	Metric	Imperial	American
Avocados	2	2	2
Lemon juice	15 ml	1 tbsp	1 tbsp
Butter or margarine, melted	45 ml	3 tbsp	3 tbsp
Salt and freshly ground black pepper			
Chopped fresh parsley	30 ml	2 tbsp	2 tbsp

Peel and stone (pit) the avocados and sprinkle with lemon juice. Cut into thick slices. Brush generously with butter or margarine and season with salt and pepper. Barbecue or grill for about 2 minutes each side until lightly browned. Serve sprinkled with parsley.

Breaded Button Mushrooms

Serves 4

	Metric	Imperial	American
Button mushrooms	450 g	1 lb	1 lb
Plain (all-purpose) flour	30 ml	2 tbsp	2 tbsp
Salt and freshly ground black pepper			
Egg, beaten	1	1	1
Fine breadcrumbs	50 g	2 oz	1 cup
Oil for deep-frying			

Dust the mushrooms in seasoned flour, shaking off any excess. Dip in the beaten egg, then in breadcrumbs until well covered. Fry (sauté) in hot oil for about 4 minutes until golden brown. Drain well on kitchen paper before serving.

ON THE GRILL

Many firm vegetables can be placed straight on the barbecue with the most wonderful results – simple barbecued onions have quite a different taste from when they are cooked in any other way. Choose firm vegetables so that they don't fall apart during cooking. Some vegetables are best par-boiled before you start so that you can ensure that melt-in-the-mouth centre and crispy outside.

Vegetarian burgers and sausages, and other similar dishes, are best cooked in a hinged wire grill so that they are held firmly together and don't fall apart during cooking.

Nutty Celeriac

Serves 4

	Metric	Imperial	American
Celeriac (celery root)	1	1	1
White wine vinegar	15 ml	1 tbsp	1 tbsp
Oil	90 ml	6 tbsp	6 tbsp
Ground walnuts	50 g	2 oz	$^1/_2$ cup

Peel the celeriac and cut it into 2.5 cm/1 in slices and boil for about 10 minutes until just tender. Drain well. Mix together the remaining ingredients and brush over the celeriac. Leave to stand for about 30 minutes. Barbecue for about 5 minutes until crispy.

Grilled Chicory

Serves 4

	Metric	Imperial	American
Chicory (Belgian endive) heads	4	4	4
Oil	30 ml	2 tbsp	2 tbsp
Butter or margarine, melted	30 ml	2 tbsp	2 tbsp
Chopped mixed fresh herbs	30 ml	2 tbsp	2 tbsp
Salt and freshly ground black pepper			

Slice the chicory in half lengthways. Mix together the oil, butter or margarine, herbs, salt and pepper and brush over the chicory. Barbecue for about 10 minutes, turning and basting with more oil mixture as it cooks.

Fennel with Caraway

Serves 4

	Metric	Imperial	American
Fennel bulbs, thickly sliced	4	4	4
Butter or margarine, melted	45 ml	3 tbsp	3 tbsp
Caraway seeds	15 ml	1 tbsp	1 tbsp
Salt and freshly ground black pepper			
Grated Parmesan cheese	50 g	2 oz	1/2 cup

Cook the fennel in boiling water for about 6 minutes until just tender. Drain well, then leave to cool. Brush the fennel with butter, sprinkle with caraway seeds and season with salt and pepper. Barbecue for about 2 minutes on each side until lightly browned. Transfer to a serving dish and sprinkle with Parmesan.

Nutty Burgers

Serves 4

	Metric	Imperial	American
Bulghar	175 g	6 oz	1 cup
Water	1 litre	1³/₄ pts	4¹/₄ cups
Salt and freshly ground black pepper			
Cornmeal	100 g	4 oz	1 cup
Peanut butter	15 ml	1 tbsp	1 tbsp
Salted peanuts, finely chopped	75 g	3 oz	³/₄ cup
Oil	45 ml	3 tbsp	3 tbsp

Place the bulghar in a heavy pan and heat gently for a few minutes until it is lightly browned, shaking the pan as it heats. Pour in 450 ml/³/₄ pt/2 cups of the water, stir well and bring to the boil. Cover and simmer for 20 minutes, stirring occasionally to prevent it sticking. Season with salt and pepper.

Bring the remaining water to the boil in a large pan, stir in the cornmeal, peanut butter, and a little salt and pepper. Cover and simmer very gently for 30 minutes, stirring frequently, until the mixture is firm and comes away from the sides of the pan. Stir in the peanuts. Leave to cool.

Mix together the cornmeal mixture with the bulghar and shape into burgers. Chill well.

Brush the burgers with oil and barbecue in a hinged wire grill for about 10 minutes until browned on all sides.

Leeks or Onions with Basil Butter

Serves 4

	Metric	*Imperial*	*American*
Leeks or onions	4	4	4
Tomatoes, halved	4	4	4
Olive oil	30 ml	2 tbsp	2 tbsp
Garlic clove, crushed	1	1	1
Lemon juice	15 ml	1 tbsp	1 tbsp
Salt and freshly ground black pepper			
For the basil butter			
Butter or margarine, softened	40 g	1^1/$_2$ oz	3 tbsp
Garlic clove, crushed	1	1	1
Chopped fresh basil	15 ml	1 tbsp	1 tbsp

Trim the leeks and cut them in half lengthways, or trim and halve the onions. Brush the leeks or onions and tomatoes with olive oil, then barbecue the leeks for about 3 minutes each side, or onions for about 6 minutes each side until just soft and lightly browned, and the tomatoes for about 2 minutes each side. Transfer to a serving dish and sprinkle with garlic, lemon juice, salt and pepper. Meanwhile, blend the butter or margarine with the garlic and basil and season with salt and pepper. Dot over the vegetables and serve.

Spiced Herb Onions

Serves 4

	Metric	Imperial	American
Small onions	450 g	1 lb	1 lb
For the baste			
Chopped fresh parsley	45 ml	3 tbsp	3 tbsp
Finely chopped spring onion (scallion)	45 ml	3 tbsp	3 tbsp
Dried mixed herbs	5 ml	1 tsp	1 tsp
Mustard powder	2.5 ml	$^1/_2$ tsp	$^1/_2$ tsp
A few drops of chilli sauce			
Salt and freshly ground black pepper			
Butter or margarine, softened	225 g	8 oz	1 cup

Mix together the seasoning ingredients for the baste and blend them into the butter or margarine. A food processor is a quick way to do this. Chill until ready to cook. Brush the onions generously with the baste, then continue to brush as you barbecue them for about 20 minutes until tender.

Barbecue Idea

Try barbecuing red onions. They have a slightly sweeter flavour and look spectacular. Use them thinly sliced into salads, too.

Grilled Garlic Peppers

Serves 4

	Metric	Imperial	American
Red, yellow or green (bell) peppers	3	3	3
Oil	90 ml	6 tbsp	6 tbsp
Garlic cloves, crushed	2	2	2
Dried thyme	5 ml	1 tsp	1 tsp
Pinch of cayenne			

Cut the peppers into quarters or large strips. Mix together the remaining ingredients and brush over the peppers. Barbecue for about 10 minutes, turning and brushing frequently with the flavoured oil.

Barbecued Peppers

Serves 4

	Metric	Imperial	American
Red (bell) pepper	1	1	1
Green (bell) pepper	1	1	1
Orange (bell) pepper	1	1	1
Yellow (bell) pepper	1	1	1
Olive oil	45 ml	3 tbsp	3 tbsp
Chopped fresh basil	15 ml	1 tbsp	1 tbsp
Salt and freshly ground black pepper			

Remove the stalk and seeds from the peppers, but leave them intact. Brush with some of the olive oil. Barbecue for about 8 minutes, turning frequently until the peppers are soft and the skin is charred. Wrap in a paper or thick plastic bag and seal the top to keep the steam inside. Leave for about 10 minutes until the peppers are just cool enough to handle. Peel off the skin and tear the peppers into strips. Place in a bowl and sprinkle with the remaining oil, the basil, salt and pepper.

Potato Wedges

Serves 4

	Metric	Imperial	American
Large potatoes, scrubbed	4	4	4
Salt			
Butter or margarine, softened	75 g	3 oz	1/3 cup
Garlic cloves, crushed	2	2	2
Chopped fresh basil	15 ml	1 tbsp	1 tbsp
Freshly ground black pepper			

Cook the potatoes in boiling salted water until just tender.
Drain and cut into large wedges. Mix the butter or
margarine with the garlic, basil, pepper and a little salt,
if liked. Brush over the potatoes. Barbecue the potatoes,
on a piece of foil if this is easier, for about 6-10 minutes
until golden.

Sweet Potatoes with Nutty Butter

Serves 4

	Metric	Imperial	American
Sweet potatoes	4	4	4
Butter or margarine	100 g	4 oz	$^1/_2$ cup
Clear honey	5 ml	1 tsp	1 tsp
Juice and grated rind of orange	1	1	1
Walnuts, chopped	25 g	1 oz	$^1/_4$ cup
Pinch of mustard powder			
Salt and freshly ground black pepper			

Pierce the skin of the potatoes and cook them in the oven at 200°C/400°F/gas mark 6 for about 1 hour until soft, or on the barbecue for about 2 hours. Melt all the remaining ingredients together in a pan and keep hot.

To serve, split open the potatoes and spoon over the flavoured butter.

Spinach-stuffed Mushrooms

Serves 4

	Metric	Imperial	American
Large flat mushrooms	8	8	8
Butter or margarine	25 g	1 oz	2 tbsp
Oil	15 ml	1 tbsp	1 tbsp
Onion, chopped	1	1	1
Garlic cloves, chopped	2	2	2
Frozen spinach, thawed and drained	225 g	8 oz	1/2 lb
Vegetable stock	90 ml	6 tbsp	6 tbsp
Salt and freshly ground black pepper			
Curd (smooth cottage) cheese	100 g	4 oz	1/2 cup
Dry breadcrumbs	45 ml	3 tbsp	3 tbsp
Parmesan cheese, freshly grated	50 g	2 oz	1/2 cup

Remove the stems from the mushrooms and chop them finely. Heat the butter or margarine and oil and fry (sauté) the onion and garlic until soft. Stir in the mushroom stalks, spinach and stock and season well with salt and pepper. Remove from the heat and stir in the curd cheese. Place the mushroom caps stem-side up and pile the mixture on top. Sprinkle with breadcrumbs and Parmesan. Barbecue for about 10 minutes until cooked through and bubbling.

Sweetcorn with Lime and Chilli Butter

Serves 4

	Metric	*Imperial*	*American*
Sweetcorn (corn) on cobs	4	4	4
Butter, softened	175 g	6 oz	³/₄ cup
Lime juice	45 ml	3 tbsp	3 tbsp
Chilli powder	10 ml	2 tsp	2 tsp
Salt			

Leave the sweetcorn in the husks. Soak in cold water for at least 20 minutes.

Beat together the butter, lime juice and chilli powder to taste and season to taste with salt. Roll the flavoured butter into a sausage shape and chill.

Drain the corn and barbecue in the husks for about 20 minutes until the husks are evenly browned. Remove from the grill and carefully take off the husks and silks. Serve with the flavoured butter cut in slices.

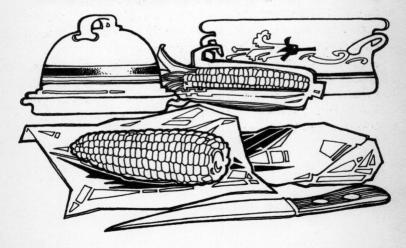

Sage and Onion Tomatoes

Substitute parsley and thyme, or any other of your favourite herbs for the sage.

Serves 4

	Metric	Imperial	American
Large tomatoes, halved	4	4	4
Salt and freshly ground black pepper			
Onion, finely chopped	1	1	1
Fresh breadcrumbs	50 g	2 oz	1 cup
Chopped fresh sage	5 ml	1 tsp	1 tsp
Strong cheese, grated	100 g	4 oz	1 cup

Scoop out the seeds from the tomato halves and season with salt and pepper. Mix the onion with the breadcrumbs and sage and season with salt and pepper. Pile the stuffing mixture back into the tomato halves and barbecue for about 5 minutes. Top the tomatoes with the grated cheese and barbecue for a further 5 minutes until melted.

Grilled Vegetables
with Peanut Mayonnaise

Serves 4

	Metric	Imperial	American
For the mayonnaise			
Garlic cloves, chopped	2	2	2
Egg	1	1	2
Peanut butter	15 ml	1 tbsp	1 tbsp
Lime juice	30 ml	2 tbsp	2 tbsp
Olive oil	120 ml	4 fl oz	¹/₂ cup
Salt and freshly ground black pepper			
Aubergine (eggplant)	1	1	1
Courgettes (zucchini)	2	2	2
Red (bell) peppers	2	2	2
Spring onions (scallions)	8	8	8
Garlic clove, crushed	1	1	1
Olive oil	120 ml	4 fl oz	¹/₂ cup

Make the mayonnaise in advance. Blend together the garlic, egg, peanut butter and lime juice in a blender or food processor. Slowly add the oil in a steady stream until the mixture thickens. Season to taste with salt and pepper. Leave to stand for a few hours before serving, if possible.

Cut the aubergine lengthways into 2.5 cm/1 in thick slices. Sprinkle with salt and leave to stand for 1 hour. Rinse and pat dry. Cut the courgettes lengthways into thick slices, quarter the peppers and trim the spring onions. Mix the garlic into the oil and brush over the vegetables. Barbecue for about 10 minutes, turning and brushing regularly, until cooked through and browned. Serve with the peanut mayonnaise.

Spinach and Cheese Patties

Serves 4

	Metric	*Imperial*	*American*
Frozen, thawed or cooked spinach	450 g	1 lb	1 lb
Strong cheese, grated	225 g	8 oz	2 cups
Salt and freshly ground black pepper			
Pinch of grated nutmeg			
Egg yolks, beaten	2	2	2
Melted butter or margarine	15 ml	1 tbsp	1 tbsp
Egg, beaten	1	1	1
Dried breadcrumbs	100 g	4 oz	1 cup
Oil			

Place the spinach in a colander and press it down to drain it thoroughly. Chop it finely. Beat in the cheese, a little salt and pepper and the nutmeg. Beat the egg yolks with the butter or margarine and stir into the mixture to bind it together. Shape into patties. Brush the patties with beaten egg and roll in breadcrumbs, pressing them on firmly until covered. Chill well.

Brush both sides of the patties with oil and barbecue in a hinged wire grill for about 10 minutes until crisp and cooked through.

Potato and Coriander Burgers

Serves 4

	Metric	*Imperial*	*American*
Potatoes	*750 g*	*1¹/₂ lb*	*1¹/₂ lb*
Split red lentils	*50 g*	*2 oz*	*¹/₃ cup*
Oil	*30 ml*	*2 tbsp*	*2 tbsp*
Cumin seeds	*2.5 ml*	*¹/₂ tsp*	*¹/₂ tsp*
Finely chopped onion	*30 ml*	*2 tbsp*	*2 tbsp*
Chopped fresh coriander (cilantro)	*45 ml*	*3 tbsp*	*3 tbsp*
Ground coriander (cilantro)	*1.5 ml*	*¹/₄ tsp*	*¹/₄ tsp*
Pinch of ground cumin			
Pinch of cayenne			
Salt and freshly ground black pepper			
Flour for dusting			
Oil for brushing			

Boil the potatoes in their skins, leave to cool slightly then peel and mash. Boil the lentils in water to cover until soft, then drain thoroughly. Heat the oil and fry (sauté) the cumin seeds for a few seconds. Add the onion, coriander and spices and fry (sauté) for 2 minutes. Stir in the lentils, season with salt and pepper and simmer, stirring frequently, until the mixture is dry. Leave to cool.

Divide each mixture into 8 pieces and shape into rounds. Press a ball of lentil filling into each ball of potato and press gently into patties. Dust with flour and chill until firm.

Brush the patties with oil and barbecue in a hinged wire grill for about 10 minutes until golden brown.

Cheesy Grilled Polenta

Serves 4

	Metric	Imperial	American
Water	900 ml	$1^1/_2$ pts	$3^3/_4$ cups
Salt	10 ml	2 tsp	2 tsp
Polenta	225 g	8 oz	2 cups
Butter or margarine	75 g	3 oz	$^1/_3$ cup
Parmesan or other strong cheese, grated	50 g	2 oz	$^1/_2$ cup
Olive oil	60 ml	4 tbsp	4 tbsp

To serve
Grated cheese
Sprigs of fresh basil

Bring the water and salt to the boil, gradually add the polenta and stir until the mixture begins to thicken. Simmer very gently, stirring occasionally, for about 20 minutes until thick. Stir in the butter or margarine and the cheese. Spoon into a Swiss roll tin (jelly roll pan) or flat-based tin so that the polenta is about 2.5 cm/1 in thick. Leave to cool, then chill.

When ready to cook, cut the polenta into squares and brush with oil. Barbecue for about 5 minutes each side until golden brown. Serve sprinkled with more cheese and sprigs of fresh basil.

KEBABS

Vegetables make wonderful kebabs. The golden rules are to choose vegetables that will take about the same length of time to cook, and to cut them into similar-sized pieces so that they cook evenly. Baste the kebabs well with oil, butter or a marinade and turn them frequently while they are cooking. The only limit then is your own imagination.

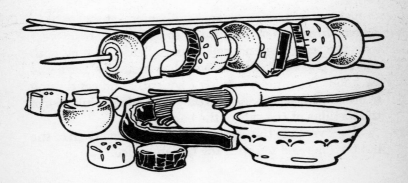

Vegetable Fajitas

Serves 4

	Metric	Imperial	American
Ripe or canned tomatoes, diced	450 g	1 lb	1 lb
Onion, finely chopped	1	1	1
Fresh green chillies, finely chopped	4	4	4
Chopped fresh coriander (cilantro)	60 ml	4 tbsp	4 tbsp
Garlic clove, crushed	1	1	1
Lime juice	30 ml	2 tbsp	2 tbsp
Salt and freshly ground black pepper			
Aubergine (eggplant)	1	1	1
Green (bell) pepper	1	1	1
Red onion	1	1	1
Cherry tomatoes	225 g	8 oz	1/2 lb
Button mushrooms	225 g	8 oz	1/2 lb
Oil	90 ml	6 tbsp	6 tbsp
Tortillas	12	12	12

Make the sauce up to 2 days in advance. Mix together the first six ingredients and season to taste with salt and pepper.

Cut the aubergine, pepper and onion into 2 cm/³/₄ in cubes. Thread alternately on to soaked wooden skewers with the tomatoes and mushrooms. Season the oil with salt and pepper and brush over the vegetables. Barbecue for about 8 minutes, turning frequently and continuing to brush with seasoned oil as they cook. Meanwhile, warm the tortillas at the side of the barbecue.

To serve, slide the vegetables off the skewers on to the hot tortillas and top with the tomato sauce.

Courgette Ribbons Vinaigrette

Serves 4

	Metric	Imperial	American
Courgettes (zucchini)	450 g	1 lb	1 lb
Olive oil	30 ml	2 tbsp	2 tbsp
White wine vinegar	5 ml	1 tsp	1 tsp
Garlic clove, crushed	1	1	1
Chopped fresh parsley	15 ml	1 tbsp	1 tbsp
Salt and freshly ground black pepper			

Use a potato peeler to cut the courgettes into long thin ribbons. Place 2-3 ribbons on top of each other then thread them on to soaked wooden skewers, folding them backwards and forwards like a concertina. Whisk together the oil, vinegar, garlic and parsley, salt and pepper. Brush over the courgettes. Barbecue for about 8-10 minutes, turning and basting frequently.

Curried Coconut Cauliflower

Serves 4

	Metric	Imperial	American
Garlic clove, crushed	1	1	1
Canned coconut milk	300 ml	$^1/_2$ pt	$1^1/_4$ cups
Desiccated (shredded) coconut	50 g	2 oz	$^1/_2$ cup
Curry powder	15 ml	1 tbsp	1 tbsp
Lemon juice	10 ml	2 tsp	2 tsp
Pinch of cayenne			
Salt and freshly ground black pepper			
Cauliflower, cut into florets	1	1	1

Place the garlic, coconut milk, coconut and curry powder in a pan, bring to the boil, then simmer for 15 minutes, stirring occasionally. Remove from the heat and add the lemon juice, cayenne, and a little salt and pepper. Transfer to a dish and add the cauliflower, stirring to coat it well. Leave to marinate for 3-4 hours.

Thread the cauliflower on to soaked wooden skewers and barbecue for about 6 minutes until just cooked but still crisp.

Mushroom and Banana Kebabs

Serves 4

	Metric	Imperial	American
Button mushrooms	225 g	8 oz	1/2 lb
Red (bell) peppers, cut into chunks	2	2	2
Large courgette (zucchini), cut into chunks	1	1	1
Firm banana, cut into chunks	1	1	1
Salt and freshly ground black pepper			
Freshly grated nutmeg			
Butter or margarine, melted	50 g	2 oz	1/4 cup

Thread the vegetables and banana alternately on to soaked wooden skewers. Season with salt and pepper, sprinkle with nutmeg and brush well with butter or margarine. Barbecue over a low heat for about 15 minutes, brushing and basting regularly, until the pepper and courgette are tender.

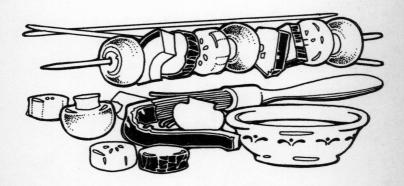

Mixed Mushroom Kebabs

Serves 4

	Metric	Imperial	American
Large mushrooms	450 g	1 lb	1 lb
Olive oil	120 ml	4 fl oz	1/2 cup
Salt and freshly ground black pepper			
Butter, melted	30 ml	2 tbsp	2 tbsp
Dry sherry	30 ml	2 tbsp	2 tbsp
Chopped fresh flat-leaf parsley	30 ml	2 tbsp	2 tbsp
To serve			
Garlic bread (see page 93)			

Toss the mushrooms in the oil with plenty of pepper until the oil is absorbed. Thread the mushrooms on to soaked wooden skewers. Barbecue the kebabs for about 8 minutes, turning frequently until crispy. Meanwhile, mix together the butter, sherry and parsley and season with salt and pepper. Arrange the kebabs in a shallow serving dish and top with the flavoured butter.

Serve with garlic bread.

Parsnip and Pepper Kebabs

Serves 4

	Metric	Imperial	American
Red (bell) pepper, cut into squares	1	1	1
Yellow (bell) pepper, cut into squares	1	1	1
Green (bell) pepper, cut into squares	1	1	1
Shallots	8	8	8
Small courgettes (zucchini), cut into chunks	4	4	4
Cooked parsnips, cut into chunks	225 g	8 oz	2 cups
For the dressing			
Soy sauce	60 ml	4 tbsp	4 tbsp
Oil	15 ml	1 tbsp	1 tbsp
Lemon juice	15 ml	1 tbsp	1 tbsp
Ground ginger	2.5 ml	$1/2$ tsp	$1/2$ tsp
Clear honey	30 ml	2 tbsp	2 tbsp

Blanch the pepper squares in boiling water for 3 minutes, then drain. Blanch the shallots in boiling water for about 5 minutes until just beginning to soften, then drain. Blanch the courgettes in boiling water for 2 minutes, then drain. Thread all the vegetables alternately on to soaked wooden skewers. Mix together the dressing ingredients and brush well over the kebabs. Barbecue the kebabs for about 10 minutes, turning and basting regularly as they cook.

Parsnip and Pears

Serves 4

	Metric	Imperial	American
Parsnips, cut into chunks	350 g	12 oz	³/₄ lb
Salt			
Pears, peeled and quartered	4	4	4
Butter or margarine	60 ml	4 tbsp	4 tbsp
Soft brown sugar	45 ml	3 tbsp	3 tbsp
Pinch of ground cinnamon			

Cook the parsnips in boiling salted water until just tender. Drain well. Thread the parsnips and pears on to soaked wooden skewers. Blend together the butter or margarine, sugar and cinnamon. Brush over the kebabs. Barbecue for about 10 minutes, turning regularly and basting with more butter or margarine as they cook.

Colourful Kebabs

Serves 4

	Metric	*Imperial*	*American*
Small aubergine (eggplant)	1	1	1
Courgette (zucchini)	1	1	1
Red (bell) pepper	1	1	1
Green (bell) pepper	1	1	1
Yellow or orange (bell) pepper	1	1	1
Shallots	4	4	4
Cherry tomatoes	8	8	8
Oil or butter			
Salt and freshly ground black pepper			

Cut the aubergine and courgette into slices. Cut the peppers into squares. Halve or quarter the shallots. Thread all the vegetables including the tomatoes alternately on to soaked wooden skewers. Brush well with oil and season with salt and pepper. Barbecue for about 10 minutes, turning frequently and brushing with more oil or butter as necessary.

Tomato and Bread Kebabs

Serves 4

	Metric	Imperial	American
White bread, unsliced and crusts removed	225 g	8 oz	1/2 lb
Cherry tomatoes	450 g	1 lb	1/2 lb
Garlic cloves, crushed	2	2	2
Olive oil	75 ml	5 tbsp	5 tbsp
Lemon juice	10 ml	2 tsp	2 tsp
Chopped fresh rosemary	15 ml	1 tbsp	1 tbsp
Chopped fresh thyme	15 ml	1 tbsp	1 tbsp
Salt and freshly ground black pepper			

Cut the bread into cubes about the same size as the tomatoes. Alternate the tomatoes and bread cubes on soaked wooden skewers. Mix together the garlic, oil, lemon juice, herbs, and a little salt and pepper. Brush generously over the kebabs. Barbecue for about 8 minutes, turning frequently and brushing with more flavoured oil as they cook.

Spring Onion and Mushrooms with Soy Sauce

Serves 4

	Metric	Imperial	American
Bunch of spring onions (scallions)	1	1	1
Button mushrooms	450 g	1 lb	1 lb
Lemon juice	60 ml	4 tbsp	4 tbsp
Soy sauce	30 ml	2 tbsp	2 tbsp
Oil	15 ml	1 tbsp	1 tbsp
Salt and freshly ground black pepper			

Cut the spring onions, green and white parts, into 2.5 cm/1 in pieces. Alternate the spring onions and mushrooms on soaked wooden skewers. Whisk together the lemon juice, soy sauce, oil, and a little salt and pepper. Brush over the kebabs. Barbecue for 4 minutes, turning frequently and brushing with more flavoured oil as they cook.

Asparagus and Lemon Kebabs

Serves 4

	Metric	Imperial	American
Quorn or smoked tofu cubes	450 g	1 lb	2 cups
Asparagus spears, cut into chunks	225 g	8 oz	1/2 lb
Lemon, thinly sliced	1	1	1
Lemon juice	10 ml	2 tsp	2 tsp
Butter or margarine, melted	50 g	2 oz	1/4 cup
Salt and freshly ground black pepper			

Thread the Quorn or tofu, asparagus and lemon slices alternately on to soaked wooden skewers. Sprinkle with lemon juice, brush with melted butter or margarine and season with salt and pepper. Barbecue for about 10 minutes until cooked through and golden.

FOIL PARCELS

Softer-textured vegetables cook very well on the barbecue in a parcel of foil, which seals in all the flavours and helps them blend together while cooking. Make larger parcels for convenience – and cook them for a little longer – or wrap the foods in individual portions for your guests to unwrap on their plates.

Italian-style Artichokes

Serves 4

	Metric	Imperial	American
Canned artichoke hearts, drained	400 g	14 oz	1 large can
White wine vinegar	15 ml	1 tbsp	1 tbsp
Chopped fresh basil	15 ml	1 tbsp	1 tbsp
Garlic clove, crushed	1	1	1
Parmesan cheese, freshly grated	100 g	4 oz	1 cup
Salt and freshly ground black pepper			

Thickly slice the artichokes and arrange them in 4 squares of foil. Sprinkle with vinegar, basil, garlic, cheese, salt and pepper. Seal the parcels and barbecue for about 15 minutes until the vegetables have heated through.

Cheese Courgettes

Serves 4

	Metric	Imperial	American
Courgettes (zucchini), thinly sliced	4	4	4
Garlic cloves, crushed	2	2	2
Olive oil	30 ml	2 tbsp	2 tbsp
Dried oregano	5 ml	1 tsp	1 tsp
Salt and freshly ground black pepper			
Emmenthal (Swiss) cheese, sliced	100 g	4 oz	1/4 lb

Arrange the courgettes on 4 pieces of foil. Sprinkle with garlic and olive oil, then with oregano, salt and pepper. Arrange the cheese on top. Seal the parcels and barbecue for about 15 minutes until the courgettes are tender and the cheese has melted.

Roasted Garlic

Serves 4

	Metric	Imperial	American
Garlic bulbs	4	4	4
Oil	60 ml	4 tbsp	4 tbsp
Butter or margarine	40 g	$1^{1}/_{2}$ oz	3 tbsp
Chopped fresh oregano	30 ml	2 tbsp	2 tbsp
To serve			
French bread			

Leave the garlic bulbs unpeeled. Slice off the tops to expose the cloves inside the skins. Place each one on a piece of foil, drizzle with oil and dot with butter or margarine, then sprinkle with oregano. Close the foil parcels and place on the side of the barbecue for about 40 minutes, opening the parcels to baste once during cooking with the flavoured oil and butter.

To serve, remove the garlic from the parcels, squeeze the cloves out of their skins and spread over French bread.

Chestnut Mushroom Parcels

Serves 4

	Metric	Imperial	American
Chestnut mushrooms, sliced	450 g	1 lb	8 cups
Spring onions (scallions), chopped	2	2	2
Garlic cloves, crushed	2	2	2
Olive oil	60 ml	4 tbsp	4 tbsp
Balsamic vinegar	15 ml	1 tbsp	1 tbsp
Chopped fresh parsley	15 ml	1 tbsp	1 tbsp
Salt and freshly ground black pepper			
Tomatoes, halved	4	4	4
Chopped fresh basil	15 ml	1 tbsp	1 tbsp

Place the mushrooms on 4 squares of foil. Sprinkle with spring onions and garlic. Whisk together 45 ml/3 tbsp of the oil with the vinegar, stir in the parsley and season with salt and pepper. Pour over the mushroom parcels and twist the foil at the top to seal. Barbecue for about 20 minutes until cooked through. Meanwhile, brush the tomatoes with the remaining oil, season with salt and pepper, sprinkle with basil and barbecue for about 5 minutes until cooked.

Mixed Vegetable Parcels

Serves 4

	Metric	Imperial	American
Small aubergine (eggplant), sliced	1	1	1
Small courgette (zucchini), sliced	1	1	1
Red (bell) pepper, sliced	1	1	1
Green (bell) pepper, sliced	1	1	1
Button mushrooms, sliced	100 g	4 oz	2 cups
Shallots, sliced	2	2	2
Cherry tomatoes	4	4	4
Garlic cloves, crushed	2	2	2
Olive oil	45 ml	3 tbsp	3 tbsp
Chopped fresh thyme	10 ml	2 tsp	2 tsp
Salt and freshly ground black pepper			

Prepare all the vegetables and divide them between 4 pieces of foil. Sprinkle with crushed garlic, oil, thyme, salt and pepper. Seal the foil parcels. Barbecue for about 25 minutes until the vegetables are tender.

Marinated Pecans

Serves 4

	Metric	Imperial	American
Pecan halves	225 g	8 oz	2 cups
Orange juice	90 ml	6 tbsp	6 tbsp
Curry powder	10 ml	2 tsp	2 tsp
Vegetarian Worcestershire			
sauce	10 ml	2 tsp	2 tsp
Soft brown sugar	5 ml	1 tsp	1 tsp
Garlic clove, crushed	1	1	1
Salt and freshly ground			
black pepper			

Mix together all the ingredients in a bowl and leave to stand for at least 1 hour. Drain the nuts and divide them between 4 pieces of foil. Seal the parcels and barbecue the nuts at the side of the barbecue for about 1 hour.

Cucumber and Onion Parcels

Serves 4

	Metric	*Imperial*	*American*
Cucumber, cut into chunks	1	1	1
Butter or margarine	50 g	2 oz	$^1/_4$ cup
Onion, thinly sliced	1	1	1
Dried mixed herbs	10 ml	2 tsp	2 tsp
Pinch of cayenne			
Salt and freshly ground black pepper			

Arrange the cucumber chunks on 4 pieces of foil and dot with the butter or margarine. Spread the onion on top, then sprinkle with the herbs and cayenne and season with salt and pepper. Seal the parcels and barbecue for about 15 minutes until the vegetables are soft.

INTERESTING EXTRAS

You need some side dishes to go with your barbecued foods, and it is usually best to prepare these in the kitchen and have them ready to serve when the main course from the barbecue is cooking and piping hot. Here is a selection of simple vegetable, rice and grain dishes, and bread ideas that offer interesting barbecue combinations.

You can also use your conventional oven to keep foods warm, especially if you have a large number of guests and a relatively small barbecue. Preheat the oven to 160°C/325°F/gas mark 3 to make sure that foods stay hot without overcooking, but do keep an eye on the foods to make sure they are still at their best. Place them on ovenproof serving plates and cover tightly with foil to maintain the moisture before placing in the oven. Don't leave them there longer than you have to.

Artichoke Cream

Serves 4

	Metric	Imperial	American
Canned artichoke hearts, drained	400 g	14 oz	1 large can
Mayonnaise (see page 108)	250 ml	8 fl oz	1 cup
Garlic clove, crushed	1	1	1
Chopped fresh basil	5 ml	1 tsp	1 tsp
White wine vinegar	5 ml	1 tsp	1 tsp
Salt and freshly ground black pepper			
Parmesan cheese, grated	75 g	3 oz	3/4 cup
Fresh breadcrumbs	25 g	1 oz	1/2 cup

Arrange the artichokes in a shallow ovenproof dish. Mix together the mayonnaise, garlic, basil, vinegar, salt and pepper and pour over the artichokes. Mix together the cheese and breadcrumbs and sprinkle over the top. Bake in the oven at 200°C/400°F/gas mark 6 for 20-25 minutes until golden.

Celery and Beans in Soured Cream

Serves 4

	Metric	Imperial	American
Celery sticks	6	6	6
French beans, trimmed	450 g	1 lb	4 cups
Olive oil	60 ml	4 tbsp	4 tbsp
Soured (dairy sour) cream	150 ml	$^1/_4$ pt	$^2/_3$ cup
Caraway seeds	15 ml	1 tbsp	1 tbsp
Salt and freshly ground black pepper			

Cut the celery into pieces the same size as the beans. Cook the celery in boiling water for about 6 minutes, adding the beans for the last 2 minutes, then drain well. Heat the oil and fry (sauté) the vegetables quickly for 2 minutes. Stir in the soured cream and caraway seeds and season with salt and pepper.

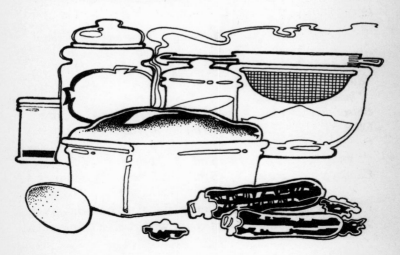

Sweet Glazed Shallots

Serves 4-6

	Metric	Imperial	American
Small shallots	450 g	1 lb	1 lb
Butter or margarine, melted	60 ml	4 tbsp	4 tbsp
Golden (light corn) syrup	60 ml	4 tbsp	4 tbsp

Peel the shallots then place them in a pan, cover with water and bring to the boil. Simmer for 4 minutes, then drain thoroughly. Arrange the shallots in a shallow baking tin (pan) and pour over the butter or margarine. Drizzle with the syrup. Cook in the oven at 200°C/400°F/gas mark 6 for about 20 minutes, stirring occasionally, until the onions are tender and golden.

Mushrooms in Balsamic Vinegar

Serves 4

	Metric	Imperial	American
Button mushrooms	450 g	1 lb	1 lb
Lemon juice	30 ml	2 tbsp	2 tbsp
Salt and freshly ground black pepper			
Balsamic vinegar	150 ml	1/4 pt	2/3 cup
Olive oil	120 ml	4 fl oz	1/2 cup
Garlic cloves, crushed	4	4	4
Chopped capers	15 ml	1 tbsp	1 tbsp
Chopped fresh parsley	45 ml	3 tbsp	3 tbsp

Place the mushrooms and lemon juice in a pan and season with salt and pepper. Just cover with water, bring to the boil, then simmer for about 5 minutes until tender. Drain. Meanwhile, bring the vinegar, oil and garlic to the boil in a separate pan. Simmer for 20 minutes. Pour the hot marinade over the mushrooms, then leave to cool. Add the capers and parsley and season with salt and pepper.

Potato Ideas

- Pre-cook jacket potatoes to save time. Pierce scrubbed potatoes with a fork and microwave for about 3 minutes per potato. Rub with a little coarse salt and oil, then wrap in foil. Alternatively, season and wrap them and cook in a hot oven at 200°C/400°F/gas mark 6 for about 1 hour. Place the wrapped potatoes directly on the barbecue coals to finish cooking.

- Offer a selection of toppings for baked potatoes: grated or crumbled cheese; pats of herb butter (see page 32); pats of garlic butter (as strong as you dare!) (see page 32); fresh tomato sauce (see page 26); even hot baked beans.

- Peel and slice potatoes and layer in an ovenproof dish, sprinkling with salt, pepper and your favourite herb as you go. Half fill the dish with milk, dot with butter and bake in the oven at 200°C/400°F/gas mark 6 for about 50 minutes until tender and the top browned.

- Peel potatoes and slice thickly, without cutting right through to the base (much as you would to make garlic bread). Slide a piece of bay leaf into each slit, sprinkle with salt and pepper and brush with plenty of olive oil. Bake in the oven at 190°C/375°F/gas mark 5 for about 1 hour, depending on size, until tender and golden.

Wild Rice Salad

Serves 4

	Metric	Imperial	American
Vegetable stock	450 ml	3/4 pt	2 cups
Wild rice	100 g	4 oz	1/2 cup
Long-grain rice	175 g	6 oz	3/4 cup
Can red pimientos, drained and chopped	400 g	14 oz	1 large can
Oil	60 ml	4 tbsp	4 tbsp
Red wine vinegar	30 ml	2 tbsp	2 tbsp
Vegetarian Worcestershire sauce	5 ml	1 tsp	1 tsp
Salt and freshly ground black pepper			

Bring the stock to the boil. Pour in the wild rice, return to the boil, cover and simmer gently for 35 minutes. Add the long-grain rice, cover again and simmer for 10-15 minutes until all the rice is cooked. If there is any liquid left, uncover and boil until absorbed. Leave to cool. Stir in the pimientos. Mix together the oil, vinegar, vegetarian Worcestershire sauce, and a little salt and pepper. Pour over the salad and toss together well.

Rice Ideas

- Rice can be used hot or cold, as the basis for a warming accompaniment, or an interesting salad.

- To save time when you guests are arriving or your family is hungry, cook long-grain rice in advance, drain it well and leave to cool. You can then use it for a quick fried-rice dish either cooked conventionally or in a frying pan (skillet) on the barbecue, or to make a rice salad.

- To make a ginger and pepper fried rice: heat a little olive oil and gently soften some chopped onion, garlic and red and green (bell) pepper. Stir in some cooked long-grain rice and 5 ml/1 tsp minced ginger and stir together until hot. Season with salt and pepper or soy sauce.

- If you are serving Eastern-inspired barbecued foods, choose a Chinese fried rice dish.

- If you like a simple side dish, cook rice in a chicken or vegetable stock to give it extra flavour.

- Add a finely pared lemon rind to the water when cooking rice, then sprinkle it with a little lemon juice and top with 5 ml/1 tsp grated lemon rind to serve.

Spiced Bulghar with Pine Nuts

Serves 4

	Metric	*Imperial*	*American*
Olive oil	*60 ml*	*4 tbsp*	*4 tbsp*
Onions, finely chopped	*225 g*	*8 oz*	*2 cups*
Garlic clove, finely chopped	*1*	*1*	*1*
Pine nuts	*30 ml*	*2 tbsp*	*2 tbsp*
Bulghar	*150 g*	*5 oz*	*scant 1 cup*
Vegetable stock	*600 ml*	*1 pt*	*2¹/₂ cups*
Salt and freshly ground black pepper			
Raisins	*30 ml*	*2 tbsp*	*2 tbsp*
Pinch of ground coriander (cilantro)			
Pinch of ground cinnamon			

Heat half the oil and gently fry (sauté) the onions until beginning to soften. Add the garlic and pine nuts and continue to fry until the onions are soft. Stir in the bulghar and remaining oil and mix well together. Add the stock and remaining ingredients, cover and bring to the boil. Simmer for about 15 minutes until all the stock is absorbed. If serving hot, stand the pan in a warm place or at the side of the barbecue for about 30 minutes until the bulghar is soft and swollen. Fluff up with a fork before serving. Serve hot or cold.

Garlic Bread

Adding parsley to the garlic butter reduces the pungency of the garlic on the breath. The amount of garlic you use is very much a matter of personal taste.

Serves 4

	Metric	Imperial	American
Garlic cloves, crushed	2	2	2
Butter or margarine, softened	100 g	4 oz	$^1/_2$ cup
Few drops of lemon juice			
Chopped fresh parsley	15 ml	1 tbsp	1 tbsp
French stick	1	1	1

Blend together the garlic, butter or margarine, lemon juice and parsley. Cut the bread in diagonal slices about 2 cm/ $^3/_4$ in thick without cutting right through the base. Spread all the cut sides of the bread with the garlic butter, then wrap the bread in foil. Place the bread in the oven at 200°C/400°F/gas mark 6 for about 20 minutes, or place at the side of the barbecue until the butter has melted into the bread and it is hot and crisp on the edges.

Vegetable Pitta Packets

Make and wrap these in advance and keep them in the warming drawer if your barbecue has one. If you like the taste of ginger, but can't be bothered with fresh, buy a jar of minced ginger to keep in the fridge.

Serves 4

	Metric	Imperial	American
Vegetable stock	300 ml	1/2 pt	1 1/4 cups
Leeks, sliced	225 g	8 oz	1/2 lb
Small apple, chopped	1	1	1
Radishes, chopped	6	6	6
Button mushrooms, sliced	4	4	4
Grated fresh ginger root	10 ml	2 tsp	2 tsp
Salt and freshly ground black pepper			
Olive oil	60 ml	4 tbsp	4 tbsp
White wine vinegar	15 ml	1 tbsp	1 tbsp
Pinch of mustard powder			
Pitta breads	4	4	4

Bring the stock to the boil in a pan, add the leeks and simmer for about 10 minutes until soft. Drain and cool. Mix together the leeks, apple, radishes, mushrooms and ginger. Season with salt and pepper. Blend together 45 ml/3 tbsp of the oil, the wine vinegar and mustard and sprinkle over the vegetables. Slit the pitta breads lengthways down one side and fill with the vegetable mixture. Brush the outsides with the remaining oil and wrap the breads individually in foil. Heat on the barbecue for about 6 minutes.

Bread Ideas

When you are in a hurry, the last thing you are likely to think about is making bread – especially when there are no end of interesting ones available in the supermarkets and bakers; we are almost spoilt for choice. Two or three tasty breads served with a barbecue add variety and interest.

- French baguettes are great – but there are lots of other possibilities. Try some of the Mediterranean-style breads with olives or sun-dried tomatoes, Italian breads such a ciabatta or pugili, or warm pitta breads. Most of these freeze well, so you can keep something in the freezer for when you need it.

- Wrap the bread in foil and warm it at the side of the barbecue to add that wonderful aroma of warm bread to the cooking.

- Rub a cut garlic clove over slices of baguette or crusty bread, then rub with the cut side of a ripe tomato (or with a tinned tomato) and sprinkle generously with olive oil, salt and freshly ground black pepper. Serve as a starter or with the meal.

- Don't forget melba toasts or any of the vast range of interesting crackers you can buy to serve as a side dish or if you are serving dips.

- If all you have is some stale bread, don't despair. Cut it thinly and toast it, then cut it into fingers to make your own crisp melba toasts. Or cut it into squares or triangles and fry (sauté) in hot oil with a dried chilli to make delicious croûtons.

SALADS

The crisp, fresh taste of a salad is the perfect complement for barbecued foods, so be imaginative and serve two or three different ones. There's a great selection here.

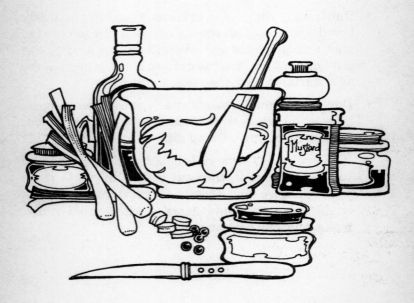

Hot Lentil Salad

Serves 4

	Metric	Imperial	American
Can green or brown lentils, drained	400 g	14 oz	1 large can
Oil	45 ml	3 tbsp	3 tbsp
Streaky bacon, cut into chunks	175 g	6 oz	1 cup
Red wine vinegar	15 ml	1 tbsp	1 tbsp
Mild mustard	5 ml	1 tsp	1 tsp
Salt and freshly ground black pepper			
Chopped fresh parsley	15 ml	1 tbsp	1 tbsp

Warm the lentils gently in a pan. Meanwhile, heat a little of the oil and fry (sauté) the bacon pieces until crisp. Blend the remaining oil with the wine vinegar, mustard, and a little salt and pepper to make a vinaigrette. Season with salt and pepper. Drain the lentils, mix with the bacon and blend with the dressing. Season again with salt and pepper to taste. Sprinkle with parsley and serve hot.

Artichoke and Sun-dried Tomato Salad

Serves 4

	Metric	Imperial	American
Can artichoke hearts, drained	400 g	14 oz	1 large can
Sun-dried tomatoes	8	8	8
Black olives, stoned (pitted)	12	12	12
Pine nuts, toasted	45 ml	3 tbsp	3 tbsp
Chopped fresh basil	30 ml	2 tbsp	2 tbsp
Lemon juice	90 ml	6 tbsp	6 tbsp
Olive oil	60 ml	4 tbsp	4 tbsp
Salt and freshly ground black pepper			

Cut the artichoke hearts into quarters and place in a bowl.
Cut the tomatoes into julienne strips and add to the
artichokes with the olives, pine nuts and basil. Blend
together the lemon juice and olive oil and season with
salt and pepper. Pour over the salad and toss well.

Crispy Fruit Coleslaw

Serves 4

	Metric	Imperial	American
Small white cabbage	1/2	1/2	1/2
Onion, grated	1	1	1
Carrot, grated	1	1	1
Eating (dessert) apple, grated	1	1	1
Raisins or sultanas (golden raisins)	50 g	2 oz	1/3 cup
Mayonnaise (see page 108)	150 ml	1/4 pt	2/3 cup
Milk	15-30 ml	1-2 tbsp	1-2 tbsp
Salt and freshly ground black pepper			

Shed the cabbage finely and place in a large bowl. Add the onion, carrot, apple and raisins or sultanas and mix well. Thin the mayonnaise with a little milk and season with salt and pepper. Pour over the salad and toss together well.

Aubergine Salad

Serves 4

	Metric	Imperial	American
Tomatoes, cut into wedges	2	2	2
Red (bell) pepper, cut into strips	1	1	1
Onion, cut into rings	1	1	1
White wine vinegar	30 ml	2 tbsp	2 tbsp
Dry sherry	30 ml	2 tbsp	2 tbsp
Oil	90 ml	6 tbsp	6 tbsp
Sesame oil	5 ml	1 tsp	1 tsp
Pinch of sugar			
Salt and freshly ground black pepper			
Aubergine (eggplant)	1	1	1
Lemon juice	30 ml	2 tbsp	2 tbsp

Mix the tomatoes, pepper and onion in a salad bowl. Mix together the vinegar, sherry, 15 ml/1 tbsp of the oil, the sesame oil, sugar, and a little salt and pepper. Pour over the salad and leave to marinate. Cut the aubergine into thin strips and toss in lemon juice to prevent discolouring. Heat the remaining oil and fry (sauté) the aubergine for about 8 minutes until lightly browned. Drain well and leave to cool. Mix the aubergine into the salad and toss together gently.

Colourful Salad

Serves 4

	Metric	Imperial	American
Green (bell) pepper, cut into strips	1	1	1
Hard-boiled (hard-cooked) eggs, quartered	2	2	2
Cucumber, thinly sliced	5 cm	2 in	2 in
Tomatoes, cut into wedges	2	2	2
Black olives, stoned (pitted)	8	8	8
Green olives, stoned (pitted)	8	8	8
Capers	5 ml	1 tsp	1 tsp
Vinaigrette (see page 109)	45 ml	3 tbsp	3 tbsp
Salt and freshly ground black pepper			

Place all the salad ingredients in a bowl and pour over the vinaigrette. Toss together gently, then season with salt and pepper.

Red Cabbage Salad

Always toss apples in a little lemon juice as soon as you have sliced them to prevent them going brown.

Serves 4

	Metric	Imperial	American
Red cabbage, finely shredded	225 g	8 oz	$1/2$ lb
Orange, peeled and cut into chunks	1	1	1
Eating (dessert) apple, cut into chunks	1	1	1
Sultanas (golden raisins)	50 g	2 oz	$1/3$ cup
Orange juice	60 ml	4 tbsp	4 tbsp
Lemon juice	15 ml	1 tbsp	1 tbsp
Clear honey	15 ml	1 tbsp	1 tbsp
Oil	60 ml	4 tbsp	4 tbsp
Salt and freshly ground black pepper			
Banana	1	1	1

Mix together the cabbage, orange, apple and sultanas in a salad bowl. Whisk together the orange and lemon juice, honey and oil. Season with salt and pepper. Pour over the salad and toss together well. Leave to stand for 2 hours. Just before serving, slice the banana and add it to the salad. Toss again and adjust the seasoning to taste.

Greek Potato Salad

Serves 4

	Metric	*Imperial*	*American*
New potatoes, cooked and diced	450 g	1 lb	2 cups
Tomatoes, chopped	225 g	8 oz	2 cups
Onion, finely chopped	1	1	1
Black olives, stoned (pitted)	50 g	2 oz	1/3 cup
Mayonnaise (see page 108)	45 ml	3 tbsp	3 tbsp
Plain yoghurt	30 ml	2 tbsp	2 tbsp
Salt and freshly ground black pepper			

Carefully mix together the potatoes, tomatoes, onion and
olives. Mix together the mayonnaise and yoghurt and
season with salt and pepper. Pour the dressing over the
salad and toss well. Chill before serving.

Cucumber and Walnut Salad

Serves 4

	Metric	Imperial	American
Cucumber, sliced	350 g	12 oz	3/4 lb
Radishes, thinly sliced	8	8	8
Green (bell) pepper, chopped	1	1	1
Spring onions (scallions), chopped	2	2	2
Walnuts, chopped	50 g	2 oz	1/2 cup
Chopped fresh parsley	15 ml	1 tbsp	1 tbsp
Chopped fresh thyme	5 ml	1 tsp	1 tsp
For the dressing			
Soy sauce	60 ml	4 tbsp	4 tbsp
Oil	15 ml	1 tbsp	1 tbsp
Lemon juice	15 ml	1 tbsp	1 tbsp
Ground ginger	2.5 ml	1/2 tsp	1/2 tsp
Clear honey, warmed	15 ml	1 tbsp	1 tbsp
Water	60 ml	4 tbsp	4 tbsp

Mix together all the salad ingredients. Whisk together the dressing ingredients. Pour the dressing over the salad and toss together well.

Feta and Cucumber Salad

Serves 4

	Metric	Imperial	American
Cucumber	1	1	1
Feta cheese, crumbled	225 g	8 oz	2 cups
Chopped fresh mint	45 ml	3 tbsp	3 tbsp
Caster (superfine) sugar	15 ml	1 tbsp	1 tbsp
Olive oil	90 ml	6 tbsp	6 tbsp
White wine vinegar	45 ml	3 tbsp	3 tbsp
Salt and freshly ground black pepper			

Slice the cucumber very thinly, using a mandoline if possible. Arrange in a shallow serving dish and sprinkle with the cheese and mint. Sprinkle over the sugar. Whisk together the oil and vinegar and season with salt and pepper. Pour over the salad and leave to stand for 1 hour before serving.

Salad Ideas

- Coarsely grate 4 or 5 carrots and season with lots of freshly ground black pepper, then dress in a simple vinaigrette dressing (see page 109), or with 45 ml/3 tbsp orange juice mixed with 15 ml/1 tbsp lemon juice; or with a yoghurt or fromage frais dressing.

- Layer sliced tomatoes with a sprinkling of sugar and snipped fresh chives, then spoon over some vinaigrette dressing (see page 109). Leave for an hour before serving, if you can.

- Dress a rinsed and drained can of mixed pulses with a vinaigrette dressing (see page 109) and sprinkle with fresh herbs.

- Mix cooked long-grain rice (about 100 g/4 oz/½ cup uncooked rice serves 4) with a selection of: chopped onion or spring onion (scallion), cooked peas, chopped mushrooms, (bell) peppers. Leave rice without a dressing, drizzle with vinaigrette (see page 109) or blend a little curry powder into 45 ml/3 tbsp mayonnaise (see page 108) and stir gently into the rice salad.

- Cook small pasta shapes in chicken stock instead of water, then drain well. Mix with diced canned pimientos, season well with salt and pepper and dress with a little vinaigrette (see page 109).

- Don't just automatically buy the same type of iceberg or round lettuce, there's loads more choice on the supermarket or greengrocers' shelves. Go for a contrast in flavours and textures; risk an unusual combination. You can choose from: little gem, lambs' lettuce, oakleaf, lollo rosso, lollo blanco, dandelion, spinach leaves, cos (romaine), Chinese leaves (stem lettuce), curly endive (chicory) – the variety is almost endless!

- To a basic potato salad of boiled new or chopped potatoes with mayonnaise (See page 108), add some chopped spring onions (scallions); freshly snipped chives; and/or a spoonful of soured (dairy sour) cream.

- Mix drained, diced cucumber into Greek yoghurt with a little clear honey and season with salt and freshly ground black pepper. Sprinkle with plenty of chopped fresh mint and serve this tzatziki as a salad or a dip.

- Mix drained canned sweetcorn (corn) with drained chopped pimientos, a chopped tomato and a few chopped mushrooms. Dress with a vinaigrette dressing (see page 109).

- Toss cubes of feta cheese with sliced onions and tomatoes and dress with olive oil and black pepper.

- Pair walnuts and sliced apples with salad leaves and a light mayonnaise (see page 108).

- Sprinkle salads with chopped nuts; chopped fresh herbs; crumbled cheese; crisply fried pieces of bacon; slivers of canned smoked mussels.

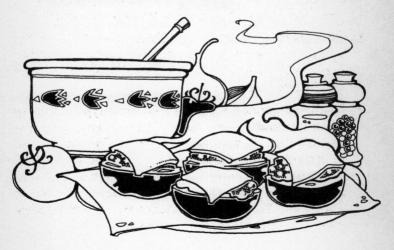

Mayonnaise

Serves 4

	Metric	*Imperial*	*American*
Egg	1	1	1
Egg yolk	1	1	1
Lemon juice	30 ml	2 tbsp	2 tbsp
White wine vinegar	15 ml	1 tbsp	1 tbsp
Mustard powder	2.5 ml	1/2 tsp	1/2 tsp
Salt and freshly ground black pepper			
Oil	375 ml	13 fl oz	1 1/2 cups

Using a blender or whisk, blend together the egg, egg yolk, lemon juice, vinegar, mustard, salt and pepper. Add a little of the oil and whisk again. Gradually add the remaining oil a little at a time, whisking or blending continuously until the mayonnaise thickens and emulsifies.

Mayonnaise Variations

To make salads dressings or dips, add one of the following to 250 ml/8 fl oz/1 cup of mayonnaise:

30 ml/2 tbsp finely chopped fresh herbs such as parsley or tarragon;

30 ml/2 tbsp finely chopped watercress, spring onions (scallions) or celery leaves;

a few crushed garlic cloves;

15 ml/1 tbsp made mustard;

15 ml/1 tbsp curry powder;

25 g/1 oz/1/4 cup crumbled blue cheese;

45 ml/3 tbsp puréed beetroot (red beet).

Vinaigrette Dressing

Serves 4

	Metric	Imperial	American
White wine vinegar	15 ml	1 tbsp	1 tbsp
Oil	45 ml	3 tbsp	3 tbsp
Mild mustard	5 ml	1 tsp	1 tsp
Salt and freshly ground black pepper			

Blend all the ingredients together well.

Vinaigrette Variations
Choose from these flavours to add to a basic vinaigrette:

    15 ml/1 tbsp chopped fresh herbs;
    15 ml/1 tbsp chopped capers or gherkins (cornichons);
    15 ml/1 tbsp chopped black or green olives.

Thousand Island Dressing

Serves 4

	Metric	Imperial	American
Tomato purée (paste)	15 ml	1 tbsp	1 tbsp
Chopped red (bell) pepper	15 ml	1 tbsp	1 tbsp
Chopped green (bell) pepper	15 ml	1 tbsp	1 tbsp
Gherkin (cornichon), chopped	1	1	1
Hard-boiled (hard-cooked) egg, chopped	1	1	1
Mayonnaise (see page 108)	150 ml	$1/4$ pt	$2/3$ cup

Blend the ingredients together well. Use as a salad dressing or dip.

Soy Dressing

Serves 4

	Metric	Imperial	American
Soy sauce	60 ml	4 tbsp	4 tbsp
Lemon juice	15 ml	1 tbsp	1 tbsp
Oil	15 ml	1 tbsp	1 tbsp
Clear honey	20 ml	4 tsp	4 tsp
Ground ginger	2.5 ml	$1/2$ tsp	$1/2$ tsp
Water	60 ml	4 tbsp	4 tbsp

Blend all the ingredients together well.

BARBECUE DESSERTS

A delicious dessert rounds off a meal nicely, especially if you are entertaining. Fruit is an excellent choice, not only because it barbecues well, but also because it offers a good taste counterpoint to a rich main course. Ice cream is always a summer favourite, especially with children, so keep some in the freezer and dress it up for the occasion.

Melon and Grapes with Brie

Serves 6

	Metric	Imperial	American
Cantaloupe melon	1	1	1
Honeydew melon	1	1	1
Watermelon	1/2	1/2	1/2
Seedless grapes	225 g	8 oz	1/2 lb
Fromage frais	90 ml	6 tbsp	6 tbsp
Brie cheese	100 g	4 oz	1/4 lb
Flaked almonds	50 g	2 oz	1/2 cup

Cut the melons into wedges, discarding the seeds and
peel, and arrange on serving plates. Arrange the grapes
on top. Place a spoonful of fromage frais at the side of
each plate. Cut the Brie into wedges and sit on a piece of
foil. Barbecue for about 30 seconds on each side until warm
and slightly runny. Place on top of the fruits. Sprinkle
with flaked almonds and serve at once.

Bananas Foster

Serves 4

	Metric	Imperial	American
Butter or margarine, melted	45 ml	3 tbsp	3 tbsp
Soft brown sugar	45 ml	3 tbsp	3 tbsp
Pinch of ground cinnamon			
Pinch of grated nutmeg			
Bananas, halved lengthways	4	4	4
To serve			
Vanilla ice cream			
Chopped mixed nuts	60 ml	4 tbsp	4 tbsp

Mix the butter with the sugar, cinnamon and nutmeg.
Brush the mixture over the bananas. Place on a sheet of
foil. Barbecue for about 5 minutes until soft and brown.
Spoon into serving dish and top with ice cream and nuts.

Gingered Melon

Serves 4

	Metric	Imperial	American
Honeydew melon	1	1	1
Finely chopped crystallised (candied) ginger	15 ml	1 tbsp	1 tbsp
Finely chopped fresh ginger root	30 ml	2 tbsp	2 tbsp
Dry white wine	120 ml	4 fl oz	1/2 cup
Ground cinnamon	5 ml	1 tsp	1 tsp
Pinch of sugar			
Pinch of salt			

Peel the melon, then cut it into wedges. Mix the crystallised and root ginger, wine, cinnamon, sugar and salt in a pan and bring to the boil. Add the melon wedges, remove from the heat, then leave to cool. Drain the melon, reserving the liquid in the pan. Boil the liquid until syrupy and reserve. Barbecue the melon wedges for about 5 minutes until lightly browned, then serve with the sauce.

Pears with Liqueur Cream

Serves 4

	Metric	Imperial	American
Pears	4	4	4
Butter or margarine, melted	45 ml	3 tbsp	3 tbsp
Light brown sugar			
For the sauce			
Fromage frais	225 g	8 oz	1 cup
Whipping cream, whipped	250 ml	8 fl oz	1 cup
Soft brown sugar	100 g	4 oz	1/2 cup
Plain yoghurt	250 ml	8 fl oz	1 cup
Coffee liqueur	90 ml	6 tbsp	6 tbsp
Pinch of grated nutmeg			

Peel and core the pears and slice them thickly or cut them into wedges. Mix the melted butter or margarine and sugar and brush over the pears. Arrange on a piece of foil. Barbecue the pears for about 5 minutes until warm. Blend together the fromage frais, cream, sugar, yoghurt, liqueur and nutmeg. Place the pears on serving plates and top with the liqueur cream.

Orange Chestnut Kebabs

Serves 4

	Metric	Imperial	American
Canned chestnuts, drained	225 g	8 oz	$1/2$ lb
Butter or margarine, melted	60 ml	4 tbsp	4 tbsp
Grated orange rind	10 ml	2 tsp	2 tsp
To serve			
Soft brown sugar	15 ml	1 tbsp	1 tbsp
Double (heavy) or whipping cream, whipped	150 ml	$1/4$ pt	$2/3$ cup

Thread the chestnuts on to soaked wooden skewers. Mix the butter with the orange rind and brush over the chestnuts. Barbecue for about 5 minutes, turning frequently and brushing with flavoured butter. Sprinkle with sugar and serve with whipped cream.

Cointreau Boats

Serves 4

	Metric	Imperial	American
Bananas in skins	4	4	4
Cointreau	30 ml	2 tbsp	2 tbsp
Demerara sugar	30 ml	2 tbsp	2 tbsp
Ground hazelnuts	30 ml	2 tbsp	2 tbsp

Barbecue the bananas in their skins for about 15 minutes until dark brown. Carefully cut off a strip of skin about 1 cm/¹/₂ in wide along the length of the banana, sprinkle with Cointreau and leave for 1-2 minutes. Sprinkle the banana flesh with sugar and hazelnuts and serve in the skins.

Chocolate Sandwiches

Especially popular with children, you can let them make up their own parcels while you are preparing the barbecue.

Serves 6

	Metric	Imperial	American
Plain (semi-sweet) chocolate	450 g	1 lb	1 lb
Marshmallows	12	12	12
Digestive biscuits (Graham crackers)	12	12	12

Break the chocolate into squares. Arrange the chocolate and marshmallows on top of half the biscuits, then top with the other biscuits to make sandwiches. Wrap individually in foil. Place the foil parcels on the barbecue for about 1-3 minutes. Serve at once.

Barbecued Fruits

Barbecuing fruits make a simple and tasty dessert.

- Arrange sliced fruits on a piece of foil, dot with butter and sprinkle lightly with sugar and a touch of cinnamon or freshly grated nutmeg. Sprinkle with a little rum or brandy, if you like. Seal the foil tightly then place on the barbecue for about 15 minutes.

- Try: thickly sliced peaches, pear halves, orange segments, pineapple rings, banana halves, sliced apples.

- Cinnamon and nutmeg are wonderful spices for sprinkling over fruit before cooking. Nutmeg is at its best if freshly grated as it loses its pungency very quickly.

- Don't ignore herbs with fruit. Those old favourites mint and rosemary go particularly well with fruits.

- Alternatively, try kebabs. Go for firm fruits such as pineapple apple, apricot, plums or kiwi fruit in different colours. Use just 2 or 3 fruits for each kebab, threading them alternately.

- Whether you are grilling or preparing as kebabs, soak fruits in a little dessert wine, red wine or your favourite liqueur for 30 minutes before barbecuing. Brush with melted butter or a little oil while they are cooking.

- You can barbecue bananas on the grill or even directly on the coals in their skins; they only take a few minutes to heat through and soften. Take great care when eating, though, as the whole thing gets very hot.

Simple Fruit Ideas

- A bowl of fresh fruit is the simplest dessert and can be quite a spectacular dish. And there's nothing better than fruit to counter the sometimes rich flavours of the barbecue.

- There's no need for a vast range of fruits: two or three choices are plenty for an impromptu occasion, so simply arrange what you have attractively in a large bowl or on a platter.

- If you are buying specially, choose just three or four fruits which offer a contrast in texture and colour to make a stunning display for your table centre which then makes a delicious end to the meal.

- Although we can now buy almost anything at almost any time of the year, choosing fruits in season usually means that you get the best value and the best quality.

- Buy one large water melon and cut it into thin crescents – deliciously refreshing if a little messy!

Fruit Salads

- A fruit salad is slightly more sophisticated. Select three or four different fruits with complementary colours and flavours. (Bananas tend to discolour and go very soft so are best saved for hot dishes.) You can use what you have available, or try the following combinations: apples, melon, kiwi fruit, raspberries; pineapple, pears, mango; peaches, plums, apricots; oranges, grapes, pineapple, apples; blackberries, apples, redcurrants.

- Remove any cores or stones (pits) from fresh fruits. Whether you peel fruit is up to you. Some pears, for example, have a tasty skin, while others are rather coarse and might spoil the salad. To peel soft-skinned fruit, such as peaches, dip them in boiling water for about 20 seconds, transfer to cold water, then peel off the skin.

- Dice the fruit neatly in equal bite-sized pieces. Always have some lemon juice handy so that you can sprinkle it over apples, peaches or pears as soon as you cut them to prevent them from discolouring. Diced fruits will create their own juice; don't waste any while you are preparing the salad, simply add it to the bowl. If you feel that the salad needs a little more liquid, add a little orange or apple juice with a dash of sherry or brandy.

- Don't forget that you can also add canned fruits if you don't have enough fresh. Buy fruits in fruit juice or a light syrup for a fresh flavour; fruits in syrup tend to be a little cloying.

- If you want to add a sugar syrup to the fruit salad, boil 275 g/10 oz/1¼ cups sugar with 600 ml/1 pt/ 2½ cups water and a squeeze of lemon juice until it is the consistency you prefer. Leave to cool before pouring over the fruit. Alternatively use pure apple or orange juice as a 'base'.

- A few fresh or frozen strawberries – sliced if they are large – or raspberries can be scattered over the top for effect. Or, if you have just one kiwi fruit left, arrange it on top of the salad, rather than mixing it in.

- Garnish the fruit salad with a few fresh mint leaves and serve it on its own, or with a little cream or crème fraîche. Ice creams and sorbets also make good accompaniments.

Ice Cream Ideas

- Dress up ordinary ice cream with a sprinkling of chopped nuts, sugar strands, chopped fresh or dried fruits or a drizzle of maple syrup, flower honey, your favourite ice cream sauce or fruit purée.

- Cut two flavours of ice cream – preferably in contrasting colours – into 1 cm/½ in cubes and serve on its own, or with similar-sized cubes of fruit.

- Layer scoops of ice cream, whipped cream, chopped nuts, toasted fresh breadcrumbs, soft fruits, fruit purée or thick sauce in sundae glasses and top each with a swirl of whipped cream.

- Plain sweet biscuits are tasty accompaniments.

Other Dessert Ideas

- Sorbets and mousses make good barbecue desserts and can be bought or made in advance and kept in the fridge or freezer. Dress them up with some grated chocolate, grated orange rind, chopped nuts, fruit purée or fruit slices, depending on the flavour.

- Poach a few ready-to-eat dried apricot halves in apple juice with a slug of white wine or sherry for 10 minutes, then leave them to soak for as long as possible. Drain and serve topped with a spoonful of cranberry sauce and a swirl of cream.

- Cold desserts are most welcome. Keep a frozen gâteau or special dessert such as a lemon tart in the freezer; it will only take a couple of hours to defrost when you decide to barbecue.

- Mix together equal quantities of strong black coffee with brandy or rum and spoon over sponge fingers or slices of sponge cake in a bowl until they are soaked. Top with lightly whisked mascarpone and sprinkle with grated chocolate.

- Pancakes with honey, sugar or maple syrup and lemon juice make a perfect dessert. Make them in advance, interleave with greaseproof (waxed) paper and reheat in the oven while you are eating the main course.

- Melt brandy snaps for a few seconds in a warm oven, then shape them into baskets to hold fruit or ice cream.

- Brush 2 or 3 squares of filo pastry with melted butter and place them one on top of each other. Place a spoonful of mincemeat or some very thinly sliced eating (dessert) apples in the centre and scrunch together to form a little purse. Brush with more melted butter. Bake in the oven at 200°C/400°F/gas mark 6 for about 10 minutes until crisp. Serve with cream.

- Dissolve 100 g/4 oz/¹/₂ cup caster (superfine) sugar over a very gentle heat until golden brown. Remove from the heat and add 60 ml/4 tbsp lemon juice and 750 ml/ 1¹/₄ pts/3 cups water. Return to the heat, bring to the boil, then simmer for 3 minutes. Leave to cool, then stir in 4 sliced oranges and chill for as long as possible, preferably 4 hours.

- As a last-minute dessert, sandwich shortcake triangles together with whipped cream and soft fruit. Top with a swirl of cream and a little grated chocolate.

- Swirl a spoonful of colourful fruit purée or sieved jam into thick plain yoghurt for a simple but dramatic dessert.

- Purée a tub of ricotta cheese with about half the quantity of drained canned peaches, then pile on slices of crusty bread or toast and sprinkle with soft brown sugar.

Drink Ideas

- For a hot outdoor meal, always make sure you have plenty of drinks and plenty of ice cubes.

- Keep the options simple: red or chilled white wine; lager or beer; soft drinks.

- Special occasion? For all but the *cognoscente*, well chilled Bucks Fizz is just as welcome made with a good sparkling wine. Mix 2 parts 'bubbly' with 1 part fresh orange juice.

- Dilute lemon squash with soda water, sweeten with a little honey and float thinly sliced lemons and ice cubes in the jug.

- Fruit juices can be heavy to serve with food. Try a mixture of orange and pineapple juice topped up with an equal quantity of soda water or sparkling mineral water.

- Make milky coffee and chill it thoroughly. Whisk in a few scoops of vanilla ice cream before serving with ice cubes.

- Herbal teas or fruit teas can be more refreshing than coffee when served after a meal on a hot day. Or offer China tea served with a slice of lemon.

INDEX

More Vegetarian Cookery from Foulsham

		QUANTITY	AMOUNT
The Complete Book of Vegetarian Recipes	0-572-02120-8 £6.99		
First Steps to a Vegetarian Family	0-572-01977-7 £4.99		
Quick & Easy Indian Vegetarian	0-572-01886-X £4.99		
Quick & Easy Students' Vegetarian Cook Book	0-572-02042-2 £3.99		
Vegetarian Microwave	0-572-01746-4 £3.99		

*Please allow 75p per book for post & packing in UK
Overseas customers £1 per book.*

* POST & PACKING

TOTAL

Foulsham books are available from local bookshops. Should you have any difficulty obtaining supplies please send Cheque/Eurocheque/Postal Order (£ sterling only) made out to BABP or debit my Credit Card:

☐ ACCESS   ☐ VISA

☐ MASTER CARD   ☐☐☐☐☐☐☐☐☐☐☐☐☐☐☐☐

EXPIRY DATE   SIGNATURE

ALL ORDERS TO:
Foulsham Books, PO Box 29, Douglas, Isle of Man IM99 1BQ
Telephone 01624 675137, Fax 01624 670923, Internet http://www.bookpost.co.uk.

NAME

ADDRESS

Please allow 28 days for delivery.
Please tick box if you do not wish to receive any additional information ☐
Prices and availability subject to change without notice.